MW00427227

Magical Places

The Story of Spartanburg's Theatres
& Their Entertainments: 1900-1950

Magical Places

The Story of Spartanburg's Theatres
& Their Entertainments: 1900-1950

Marion Peter Holt

For Evelyn,
with many good wishes,

Marion Peter Holt

9/9/04

2004

Copyright ©2004 by Marion Peter Holt

All rights reserved. No part of this book may be reproduced in any form or by any electronic or mechanical means including information storage and retrieval systems without permission in writing from the publisher, except by a reviewer, who may quote brief passages in a review.

ISBN 1-891885-36-7
First printing, August 2004

Title page photograph: A night shot of the Strand, showing a Humphrey
    Bogart film, in 1941—*Courtesy, Tommy Acker*
Front cover photograph: The Carolina Theatre at night, 1938 or 1939
    —*Courtesy, Ambrose Hudgens & the Spartanburg County Regional Museum*
Back cover photo collage: Various period Spartanburg newspaper ads
Cover and book design: Mark Olencki
Editors: Betsy Wakefield Teter & Pamela Ivey Huggins
Printed by: McNaughton & Gunn, Inc., Saline, MI

Holt, Marion Peter.
  Magical places : the story of Spartanburg's theatres and their
  entertainments, 1900-1950 / by Marion Peter Holt.
      p. cm.
  Includes bibliographical references and index.
  ISBN 1-891885-36-7 (pbk. : alk. paper)
  1. Theaters—South Carolina—Spartanburg—History—20th century. 2.
Motion picture theaters—South Carolina—Spartanburg—History—20th
century. 3. Performing arts—South Carolina—Spartanburg—History—20th
century. 4. Motion pictures—South Carolina—Spartanburg—History—20th
century. I. Title.
  PN2277.S63H65 2004
  792'.09757'29—dc22
                          2004003877

Hub City Writers Project
Post Office Box 8421
Spartanburg, South Carolina 29305
(864) 577-9349 • fax (864) 577-0188

Dedicated to the memory of
Mary Baugham,
the longtime librarian at Spartanburg's
Kennedy Free Library on Magnolia Street
where my search through dusty volumes
of faded newspapers began. Her welcome
was understanding and constant.

The Hub City Writers Project gratefully acknowledges the support of the following sponsors who helped make this publication possible.

Arthur Cleveland
James Cobb
(in honor of his great uncles, Max and Isaac Greenewald)
Mary Jane Sanders
(in honor of her father, Robert Talbert)

~ Table of Contents ~

Preface

When I was about three years old, my mother took me with her one afternoon to a matinee. Apparently, I watched the feature film without complaint, but after seeing my first cartoon, I protested that I wanted to see more and had no desire to leave the theatre. This was the beginning of a lifelong romance with plays, operas, movies, and the magical places where one goes to see them. The year I finished Spartanburg High I got my first job as an usher at the most glamorous theatre in town, the Carolina (née the Montgomery) and soon came to know every detail of its interior. While a student at Wofford College, I discovered the dusty bound copies of *The Spartanburg Journal* and *The Spartanburg Herald* and their record of theatres, performances, and events that were so much a part of local life for more than a half-century. There was so much more than I had ever imagined, and many evenings I would go to the Kennedy Free Library on Magnolia Street and write down the dates, descriptions of new theatres that had been built, and even quotes from the surprisingly apt performance reviews that appeared at the beginning of the twentieth century. It was an ongoing pastime that no doubt seemed an eccentric hobby to some, and it was a pastime in which I grew increasingly fascinated by a departed era of cultural life that was rapidly receding in local memory.

Finally, recognizing the value of the material I had collected over the years on Spartanburg's theatrical history, I compiled much of my research into a brief (and incomplete) history of local theatres and entertainments that I placed in local libraries and the Spartanburg County Historical Society in 1991 (slightly revised in 1996) for the benefit of future historians and ordinary theatre buffs who were curious about the city's past and its lost buildings. Now, I have decided to expand my original account to include considerable additional information obtained in the past decade and a more detailed account of what Spartans actually saw in their theatres, the people who managed and worked there, as well as a consideration of the social and economic impact of live professional theatre and motion pictures over the first half of the twentieth century. In addition to a more complete story of stage entertainments and the era of coexistence between stage and screen, information is provided on several short-lived theatres, and the catalogue of plays, musicals, and vaudeville shows has not only been lengthened but also supplies the identity of a number of playwrights or collaborators that may not have been included in original newspaper ads. While I have focused on the half-century when touring had reached its peak and then began a decline to coexist with motion pictures and radio, I have added a section that chronicles the impact of television, the closing of downtown theatres, the evolution of live performance, and the revival of theatre in new forms in the United States.

In addition to extensive personal exploration of five of Spartanburg's theatres, anecdotes and facts recounted by a number of people who were either audience or theatre employees, and local newspapers and city directories, my sources have included Joseph M. McLaughlin's brief mimeographed booklet of reminiscences of people and places (*Spartanburg: 25, 30, 50 Years Ago*, 1964) and *Julius Cahn's Official Theatre Guide* (Vol. 6, 1901-1902; Vol. 7, 1902-1903; Vol. 15, 1910-11), which documents names of employees at the Opera House and provides details on stage facilities and seating capacity for both the Opera House and the Harris Theatre. The Sanborn Insurance Maps of Spartanburg have enabled me to locate specifically the sites of several short-lived theatres and to establish the basic design of the Opera House and the Harris Theatre and the approximate sizes of almost all the many theatres that opened over the years. Phillip C. Lewis's book, *Trouping: How the Show Came to Town*, has been of considerable help in understanding the booking and presentation of entertainments in the United States in the early twentieth century. Willia Estelle Daughtry's book, *Vision and Reality*, on her famed relative, Matilda Sissieretta Joyner Jones, has given me a deeper appreciation of the gifted "Black Patti," whose Troubadour company was one of the most remarkable shows to appear at both the Opera House and the Harris. Arthur Hobson Quinn's two volume *A History of the American Drama* has been useful in identifying the authors and subject matter of many now-forgotten plays and musicals that played at the Opera House and the Harris Theatre, and Gerald Bordman's *American Musical* Theatre (3rd edition) has been an indispensable reference for information on several productions. The Divine Sarah, by Arthur Gold and Robert Fizdale, has provided firsthand details on Bernhardt's performance of *Aux Champs d'Honneur* during her 1917 American tour (which included Spartanburg). The Internet Broadway Database has made it possible to identify many actors whose names are now unfamiliar and to trace the careers of several of the participants in the all-soldier show *You Know Me Al* at the Harris. I am grateful to theatre organ specialist Michael Hopson for detailed information on the theatre organs installed at the Strand and Rex and to various websites for new details on theatre organs and photoplayers, southern theatres, entertainers, the Paramount-Publix theatres, and the Wilby-Kincey company.

I am indebted to many for friendship, tolerance, and encouragement. I must pay special tribute to several people who triggered my interest in a lost past, sharing their experiences and memories as audience or employees in the theatres. It was the usually gruff George Spillers, head projectionist at the Carolina, who revealed to a teenage usher that the first movie theatre in Spartanburg had been the Magic, on Magnolia Street, and that his long career had begun there. Pullman (Pop) Ramsay, the guardian of the machinery that kept the Carolina running and supervisor of its art shop, taught the same teenage usher the tricks of the lighting board backstage and the exact speed to pull the front curtain at the beginning and end of feature films. He also was a raconteur who knew about all that had transpired behind the scenes. Louisa Carlisle, the longtime librarian at Converse College, delighted me with her vivid recall of seeing as a teenager the performance of the crippled but still mesmerizing Sarah Bernhardt at the Harris Theatre. My own father, Perry West Holt, who mispronounced the stage soubriquet of Sissieretta Jones, recounted the amazement he had felt on seeing the remarkable (and tragic) "Black Patti" and her company of African-American performers at the Harris. I am grateful to Kerr McBride, former manager of the Palmetto theatre and other theatres in the Carolinas, for his friendship and support from the days of the Spartanburg Fine Film Committee to the present, and to Jack Robison, the last manager of the State, who respected my fascination with theatres and gave me free run of his theatre. The late Dave Garvin, Jr. of Greensboro, a Wofford graduate of 1938 who was manager of the Strand at the beginning of his career, graciously shared with me his memorabilia and personal recollections at a time of great bereavement for him and his family. Dan Austell, of Winston-Salem, who also began his career in Spartanburg at the Strand and Criterion, shared his memories with great cordiality when I contacted him. Jamie Cobb, the great nephew of Spartanburg's pioneer theatre impresarios, Max and Isaac Greenewald, has aided me immeasurably by sharing his memories of his remarkable great uncles and by providing priceless photographs of them for this book. Mary Jane Sanders has generously shared her memories of her father, Robert Talbert, who managed the operations of the Carolina

Theatre for more than three decades. I owe a particular debt to Donna Turner Williams, who discovered my earlier story of Spartanburg's theatres and encouraged me to undertake the new version for publication. Others without whose help this story could not be told as fully are: the late Lionel Lawson, Carlos Moseley, Wofford College historian Phillip Racine, Oakley Coburn (dean of the library at Wofford College), Converse College historian Jeffrey Willis, Carolyn Creal (curator of the Spartanburg County Regional Museum of History), Betsy Teter and Pamela Ivey Huggins (editors at the Hub City Writers Project), David Rush (archivist at Lockwood Greene) who provided me with invaluable copies of the original architectural drawings for the Montgomery theatre, and Allison Cook, who assisted in the search through microfilm for new titles for the catalogue of performances.

—M.P.H

The Spartanburg Opera House was located on the western end of Morgan Square. The theatre auditorium was on the second floor, above the post office. The building was razed in 1907 after the close of the spring theatre season. —*Courtesy, Wofford College*

~1~

The Lure of the Stage

By the end of the nineteenth century, virtually every town in the United States with a population 5,000 or more had a theatre for professional live entertainment. They were euphemistically called "Opera Houses" or "Academies of Music," even though operas were rarely performed on their stages. What their audiences did see was a varied fare of melodramas, comedies, musical reviews, minstrel shows, and an occasional play by Shakespeare or a Restoration dramatist. With the growing railroad connections and a new Opera House at the western end of Morgan Square, Spartans saw their first professional theatre performances in the 1880s. Designed in the Victorian civic style of architecture that proliferated in the United States after the Civil War, the theatre-post office, with its soaring clock tower, dominated the city's business center for a quarter century. Although the 700-seat auditorium could not attract the likes of Edwin Booth, who appeared at Charleston's Academy of Music and theatres in Savannah, Macon, and Atlanta, it did quickly offer a variety of entertainment, sometimes selling out every seat and providing standing room for the overflow. Within a decade, gaslights had given way to electricity, making stage presentations even more appealing to local audiences.

On cold nights in January and February, the theatre's central heating could be as big a draw as the play or musical show of the evening. Undoubtedly, patrons felt that they were visiting a somewhat magical world when they entered the auditorium—the walls decorated in red and the ceiling blue, with rows of electric bulbs (a marvel that most did not yet enjoy in their own homes). Whether sitting in the prime seats of the Dress Circle or in the back row of the balcony, audiences felt a sense of enchantment and expectation when the painted front curtain rose. For more than two decades, pedestrians walked to the western end of Morgan Square to study the posters conspicuously placed on a "stand," a large poster display board located at street level under the clock tower.

Although ticket prices for a play or musical show at the Opera House (usually 75 cents to $1.50) may seem modest a century later, they were not within the reach of all Spartans. Some had to be satisfied with the street parade in which the musicians of the frequent minstrel shows provided a taste of the evening's performance for

free. That in itself was, however, a kind of theatrical happening that no doubt whetted the appetite for a second helping. If the minstrel parade lacked the elephants, tigers, and calliope music of the more exotic parades by visiting circuses, the costumed actors, strutting to the

Max Greenewald, impresario of the Opera House in its later seasons
—*Courtesy, James D. Cobb*

accompaniment of brass, drums, and cymbals, had their own magical effect on those of all ages who stopped to watch.

At the beginning of the new century, Max Greenewald, a handsome, slender young man with a dark mustache, was the local impresario (as well as a leading retailer), and it was he who decided which of the scores of shows touring the Southeast would actually come to town. Max, born in Philadelphia in 1870, moved with his family to Wilmington, North Carolina, at the age of eight. In the last decade of the nineteenth century, he arrived in Spartanburg to join his brothers in the prospering Greenewald clothing business on Morgan Square. A talented musician himself and a lover of the arts, it is not surprising that he was drawn to the theatre. He was also an exceptionally shrewd businessman who understood the tastes of local audiences, but he occasionally risked loss by booking a show that might appeal only to the most sophisticated public.

In the early 1900s, Max Greenewald's brother, Isaac, joined his family in Spartanburg and began to assist in the operation of the Opera House. Isaac's unusual background qualified him to make a major contribution to the city's theatrical life for many years. In 1886 and 1889, he had studied piano at the New England Conservatory of Music, and he had served as musical

Isaac Greeenwald, manager of the Harris Theatre in its early years
—*Courtesy, James D. Cobb*

director for a vaudeville company performing in the Northeast. Later he had taught music in Wilmington and had been the organist for the Catholic church there.

The business manager employed by the Greenewalds to oversee the day-to-day operations and keep books at the Opera House was Charles P. Ligon, and other local people officially employed or retained by the theatre were L. J. Blake (house physician), S. T. McCravy (attorney), Miss L. B. Neel, who was in charge of "typewriting," and a billposter. There were, of course, several stagehands (known then as "stage carpenters"), musicians, and maintenance personnel to help the show go on. Tickets were conveniently on sale at Greenewald's clothing store further up on the square. Since Max had leased and operated Spartanburg's first showplace for several years, it was often referred to as "The Greenewald Opera House," even though it was located in a municipal building that included the post office.

From the start, the local entertainment palace had been an economic boon to the small but growing city. Some touring shows moved on immediately after their performance to their next destination, but other actors and company personnel stayed at nearby hotels and ate at downtown cafes, particularly when a company came for a week to present its full repertory. Although acting was a suspect profession—and

Opera House
Wednesday Evening, Mch. 14

THE SOCIETY and MUSICAL EVENT
OF THE SEASON.
Appearance of

Mme. Mantelli
The Celebrated
MEZZO-SOPRANO
Formerly of the Metropolitan Opera
House, New York, and her

English Grand Opera Co.
In a complete production of

"IL TROVATORE"
The Company is Composed of Such
Well Known Artists as
Signor Aliberti, Mme. Nobli. Albrecht
De Costa, Franciseoni, Koch, Cavendish,
Aragna, etc.
Seats Now on Sale at Greenewald's.
PRICES:
Dress Circle (2 rows center) $2.00
Dress Circle (Balance) $1.50
Parquet $1.00
Gallery .. ..75c.

Opera House
Monday Night, March 12
Farewell Tour
MELVILLE B. RAYMOND
Cartoon Comedy
Buster Brown
60 — — — PEOPLE — — —60
With MASTER GABRIEL.
Talented and Well Drilled Chorus.
——SEE——
RAYMOND'S SCOTCH FUSILEERS.
A tremendous sensation in all the
Metropolitan cities.
Sale of seats starts Thursday, March
8, at 9 a. m.
Prices for this Engagement:
Dress circle, $1.50; Parquet, $1.00..
Gallery, 75 cents.

Opera House
ALL THIS WEEK
SATURDAY MATINEE
at 3:15 p. m.
Return of the Favorites
The Crescent
Comedy Co.
CHANGE OF PLAY
NIGHTLY
NEW MUSIC. NEW SPECIALTIES.
ENTIRELY NEW REPERTOIRS.
Popular Prices .. .. 10, 20 and 30 cts.
SEAT SALE AT GREENEWALD'S.
Except Friday Night

1906 ads for Opera House performances

considered nothing short of sinful by the more conservative citizens—many young Spartans eagerly took advantage of opportunities to appear as supers to fill up the stage in crowd scenes.

Touring was at its peak in the United States in 1905, and larger musical shows were coming into vogue. More than 300 different companies originated in New York alone, and many others were cast in Chicago, while others simply reappeared with a popular play dominated by a mesmerizing actor. These were appearing in cities large and small from New England to California, and theatre was a national passion even in remote mining towns. The replacement of the Opera House in 1907 by a new and much larger theatre should not seem surprising, for its auditorium was too small for a town that had tripled in size, and its stage equipment was now outdated for the increasingly elaborate touring productions. Typical of such shows was the tuneful *The Sultan of Sulu*, which played on September 25, 1906. This musical was one of the rare Chicago triumphs that had moved on to great success in New York in 1902. Its farcical plot about Ki-Ram, the island ruler who confronts the U.S. Navy, American colonialism, and a stern woman judge he tries to add to his harem, was designed solely to amuse; but its score by Alfred G. Wathall was considered one of the best of its time. Certainly, it provided the perfect excuse for colorful costumes as well as female dancers and a male chorus.

The final season at the old house was full and well attended—and it possibly even included an opera (*Parsifal*) on January 24. Although there was an early curtain with trumpet fanfare, this production was more likely only a dramatic pageant derived from Wagner's long opera about the Holy Grail. In those early years of the twentieth century, most of the plays reviewed in *The Herald* included pithy observations on dramatic content, acting, and audience reaction. The local critic, Charles Hearon, wrote: "'The Sweetest Girl in Dixie' was not as sweet to the audience as the press agent had pictured her. Though she was an actress of ordinary ability still the play would distract from the ability of any actress or actor." He went on to say, "One trouble with the play was that the old customary melodrama lines were there. 'I will not sell myself for gold,' 'Tell me about my brother,' both have been spoken here about thirty times this year..." In *The Men of Jimtown*, "there was enough powder burnt to last a whole regiment a week and if all who were killed on stage had to be buried in this town, the city limits would have to be extended..."

While the bookings in the Opera House's final season were quite varied, many of the plays were already familiar to the Spartanburg public. *East Lynne*, the epitome of nineteenth-century melodrama, was already more than forty years old when it returned to the Opera House in 1907; yet audiences loved it, and the house sold out, including standing room. Local audiences also responded favorably to the frequent musical shows. A rousing but now forgotten song called "Hinky-Dee," sung by a white actor in blackface, had Spartans applauding enthusiastically for encore after encore when the variety show *Gay New York* came to town that spring. They got their encores and surely went home happy. As it turned out, Spartans were responding to the hit song exactly as New Yorkers had when it was encored at the Murray Hill theatre the year before.

In March, audiences packed the theatre for a performance of the controversial, passion-stirring play *The Clansman*, and the critic noticed that one young woman seated on the first row of the orchestra dress circle could scarcely restrain her emotion. "She gripped the railing with fierce clutch and her face was drawn and rigid. And when a climax came she raised herself up as though about to jump forward." The next day *The Herald* published an interview with Confederate veteran Colonel Frank West, who had also been in the audience. Having personally experienced the Civil War and Reconstruction, he avowed that the play had been a thrilling and accurate portrayal of the "Old South"—except for one detail: as far as he knew, there had been no "ladies" connected with the Ku Klux Klan. He did not, to be sure, comment on the play's denigrating portrayal of African-Americans in the aftermath of slavery. Eight years later, D.W. Griffith would film *The Clansman* as *The Birth of a Nation* and the controversy did not abate even as the motion picture became an acknowledged masterpiece.

Probably the most memorable evening of theatre that spring was not at the Opera House but in the outdoor theatre at Converse College, where the popular Ben Greet Players performed Shakespeare's *Twelfth Night*. In the cast were Sidney Greenstreet as Sir Toby Belch and a radiant young English actress named Sybil Thorndike as Viola. The local critic proved his worth this time indeed, for he predicted that Miss Thorndike would go on to a great career. Decades later, Greenstreet would become a movie immortal as "the fat man" in *The Maltese Falcon* and in memorable character parts in *Casablanca* and many other films. To add to the cultural riches that spring were a solo recital by diva Marcella Sembrich and a performance of Verdi's *Requiem* by leading opera singers during the annual Southeastern Music Festival in Converse College's acoustical marvel of an auditorium.

The audiences at the Opera House included Spartans of all ages and social background. Many, of course, lived within walking distance of the theatre, in residential neighborhoods (now mostly vanished) that were close to the square, and by 1900, others could come from outlying areas on the several streetcar lines. For women, theatre attendance in the first years of the twentieth century was complicated by the fashions of the time. Full skirts skimmed the floor (as well as the mud or dust in the streets), sleeves were puffed and wrist-length, and under it all was a plethora of undergarments. To top it off (literally) were the enormous hats that had to be checked or held in the lap; moving up the stairs to the auditorium and making one's way between the rows of seats required controlling considerable fabric—as did simply sitting down. Few could even imagine the liberating revolution in style that would occur over the next two decades.

Most of the plays and musicals that played the Opera House at the turn of the century are now all but forgotten. Some exist as titles in theatre history books, and a few (like *East Lynne*) have become symbolic of the excesses of their genre. Likewise, contemporary theatregoers rarely recognize the names of most of the actors, singers, and dancers who performed across America, even though many enjoyed enormous popularity during their often long careers, and their names were sufficient to fill every seat. For example, the popular comic actor Henry E. Dixey brought his recent Broadway hit, *Facing the Music*, to the stage of the Opera House in 1903, giving local audiences a taste of what was the best in comic musicals in that year. But even a performer as admired as Dixey was destined to leave little behind to testify to his talent. Talking pictures would add longevity to many of the musicals and operettas that would come to Spartanburg in later years; their songs would still be irresistible even if their plots were clichéd. Only in occasional films, such as *Broadway to Hollywood* and *Yankee Doodle Dandy*, has there been a reasonably accurate re-creation of stage performance in the earliest years of the twentieth century.

The last performance in the Opera House was on April 17, 1907, and the next month the theatre came down. The Masonic Order bought the property for $5,500, and Spartanburg lost a distinctive landmark. The city was not, however, without a theatre to begin the fall season. Already the Harris Theatre, on the southeast corner of St. John and North Church streets, was under construction, and the progress was reported enthusiastically in both *The Herald* and *The Journal*—fortunately with details about the dimensions and architectural design that enable us to have some idea of the interior of the city's largest downtown theatre. When the new "opera house" finally opened on the night of October 7, 1907, it was an event unequaled in the experience of the more than a thousand ticket holders and one that would never again be repeated in Spartanburg. It was the peak of an era of live entertainment, and almost no one imagined that the small

The Harris Theatre stood on the southeast corner of Church Street and what is now St. John Street. In this photo, from about 1918, the LeRue Brothers, a vaudeville act, was performing. —*Courtesy, Spartanburg Herald-Journal*

Magic and Fairyland nickelodeons, which had just opened on Magnolia Street, presaged a new era of motion pictures.

The first night at the Harris was front-page news, reported more thoroughly than any other event in local theatre history. Although it was raining in torrents, a crowd had gathered on the sidewalk in front of the Harris's narrow entrance by early evening. Some arrived on foot from their nearby homes on Church Street; others came by streetcar from Pine Street; and some drove up in open automobiles that coughed and spat exhaust smoke. The performance was prefaced by speeches by the owner, J. T. Harris, and by John B. Cleveland, who sat in the opposite stage box from Harris. Harris spoke as a theatre promoter and a businessman, pointing out the suitability of the house for any show touring the South and noting pointedly how the new building had increased real estate values on North Church Street. Cleveland "spoke in a clear and firm voice, and his every word was heeded." When he finished his tribute to Harris, the audience "rose en masse," and "for a brief moment there was a silence, and then as the lights flashed there rose a mighty encore." The huge, painted drop curtain then went up on Reginald DeKoven's operetta, *The Red Feather*, the largest production most in the audience had ever seen. As the reporter of the night told it next day in *The Journal*:

> Miss Sheridah Simpson as "Red Feather" was a polished actress. Her strong rich voice was well suited to the part of the leading lady, and her facial expressions as she went through the lively melodies betrayed a winsomeness that captivated the audience. Her costumes were elegant, and she was as graceful in the role of "Red Feather," dressed in tights, as she was as the countess with her trailing skirts in a drawing room. Sarah Edwards as "Anita," a Spanish girl, was one of the cleverest little impersonators ever seen in the glow of the footlights. She was encored again and again . . . Charles Fitz, as a waiter, was without doubt the best male impersonator ever seen in Spartanburg. He was forty men in one, ranging from a waiter in a café to the presiding officer at a convention of conspirators. Speaking of this convention of conspirators, the scene effect of red light and velvet black costumes bordered with red, was the most weird sight that one could imagine ...

The reporter went on to describe the important contribution of the male chorus, "men of superb physique" in "shining corselets and golden eagles on their helmets." As for the chorus girls, they were pretty, and their acting and singing was above average." The finale of the performance offered the rousing happy ending that we expect from operetta:

> The curtain rang down on the grand finale when the trumpets were in full blast rendering the "March of the Victors," the chorus had just sung "Farewell, a Long Farewell," and "Red Feather" was locked in the arms of her lover, who had discovered the robber and countess to be one and the same.

Apparently, stage manager Joseph Hill supervised the many changes of scenery without a hitch—no doubt with a crew of stagehands from the old Opera House and a few new ones hired because of the demands of the larger theatre. Like most theatres, the Harris provided an economic boon to Spartanburg with new jobs and enhanced real estate values. Hotels also profited when an acting company stayed over. Rooms at the Finch, the Spartan Inn, and the Argyle were two dollars and up per night. Smaller establishments

Sissieretta Jones, known as "Black Patti," performed at the Harris in 1907, 1913, and 1915.
—*Courtesy, author's collection*

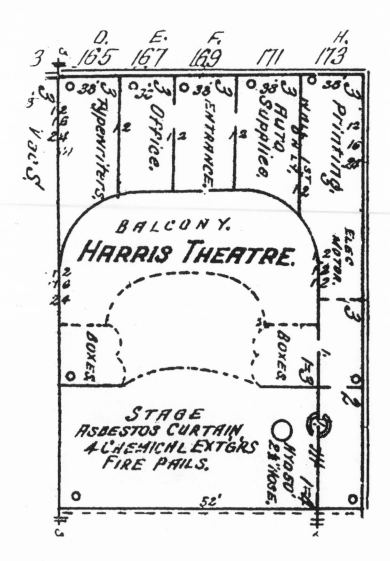

The Sanborn Insurance Map illustrates the basic design of the Harris, with stage boxes and large curving balcony and gallery. —*Courtesy, Wofford College*

such as the Magnolia and Mr. Wood's Hotel charged only a dollar.

The fortuitous narration of opening night at the Harris by a local reporter is the most vivid surviving description of a professional stage performance in Spartanburg in the early years of the twentieth century. While this night was a special celebratory event, it was not necessarily atypical in the degree of excitement it stirred up in the audience. The second performance of that opening week is also of particular interest. It was the initial appearance at the Harris of the now legendary "Black Patti," Sissieretta Jones, and her musical troupe in a show featuring "coon songs, ragtime, and horseplay." Not mentioned in the newspaper ad, but well known to ticket buyers, was the fact that the performance also had a generous sampling of operatic arias and ensembles. A daughter of slave parents, Jones had received a musical education in Rhode Island, had achieved considerable fame in Europe, and had sung at the White House and Carnegie Hall; but her race had excluded her from the stage of the Metropolitan. Her soubriquet was sometimes pronounced "Pat-eye" by those who did not understand the connection with the famed Italian-American diva Adelina Patti.

On the night of Sissieretta Jones's first Harris appearance, both first and second balconies were reserved for "coloured people." When she returned to the Harris for her third engagement, on January 10, 1913, the change in the areas of the house available to African-American patrons is noteworthy: this time the entire theatre except the left side of the orchestra was reserved for "coloured people." After her performances, Mme. Jones and her troupe returned to their private railroad car on a siding nearby. Barred from local hostelries because of their race, often the company would move on to the next booking during the night. Perhaps Sissieretta Jones did receive admirers in her dressing room or at the stage door, and no doubt some whites defied conventions and warmly shook the jeweled hand of the greatest African-American classical singer of the time. By coincidence Isaac Greenewald, manager of the Harris, and Mme. Jones had both been music students in Boston in 1886, at the New England and the Boston Conservatories of Music respectively.

The third and final show of that opening week was Sheridan's *The Rivals*, with Joe and William Jefferson, sons of Joseph Jefferson of Rip Van Winkle fame. Then, on October 12, Shakespeare's *Richard III* played to a far smaller audience. Classical plays would be a rarity at the theatre, but occasionally there were surprises. Isaac Greenewald booked the first season, no doubt with Max's input, and continued as the manager of the Harris for several years. The new theatre provided a large stage that could accommodate far more elaborate productions than before seen at the Opera House, and with roughly twice the capacity of the old house, the potential for profit was increased. No one realized that touring had already reached its peak and that a decline would set in very soon. Still, from 1907 until the end of World War I in 1918 the Harris would provide Spartanburg with an array of live entertainment, only rarely venturing into the domain of movie theatres—most notably with the first showing in the city of Griffith's *The Birth of a Nation*, with orchestra accompaniment. There were, to be sure, non-theatrical appearances at the theatre. In December 1907, the perennial Democratic presidential candidate, William Jennings Bryan, spoke from the Harris stage. In 1913, a demonstration of Thomas Edison's early talking pictures proved a curiosity but not a convincing alternative to silent films.

Stage attractions included extravaganzas such as *The Garden of Allah* ("100 people, train of eight cars, arabs, camels, horses, donkeys, goats"), the immensely popular operettas *Princess Pat* and *The Serenade* of Victor Herbert, Lehar's *Gypsy Love*, Belasco's western melodrama *The Girl of the Golden*

Harris Theatre **Friday Night October 19**

Seat Sale Opens Tuesday

For the Liebiers Co.'s Stupendous Spectacle of

100—PEOPLE—100

THE **GARDEN** OF **ALLAH**

ARABS
CAMELS

Horses
Donkeys
Goats
The Eighth
Wonder of
The World

Traveling in Its Own Special

Train of Eight Cars

Special Excursions on All Railroads

Prices:— $2, $1.50, $1, 50c.

West, and many nights of Keith Vaudeville. Theatre was continuing to provide steady employment for many Spartans both inside and outside the Harris. All the shows arrived by train, and since the Columbia line of the Southern Railway crossed Elm Street just behind the theatre itself, it is likely that the cars carrying the actors and the scenery (and in the case of *The Garden of Allah*, the animals as well) were shunted to a siding nearby. Transporting it all to the stage—sometimes only hours before the curtain went up—was laborious, often requiring the services of a local transport company.

A unique evening was the appearance on January 9, 1917, of the dauntless tourer Sarah Bernhardt, performing scenes from *Camille* and other specialties from her repertoire such as *Aux Champs d'Honneur*. Bernhardt arrived in town in her private railroad coach from Charlotte, where she had been a sensation the night before, and she was carried inside the theatre in her sedan chair. When the house lights dimmed and the footlights came up, a young bilingual American, Margaret Mower, stepped before the curtain to explain the essence of the scene that Mme. Bernhardt would then perform in French. The famed actress was already seated onstage when the curtain rose, since the amputation of a leg had limited her movement, but her voice retained the power to captivate audiences unfamiliar with the language she spoke. At the age of seventy-two, she put on a bloodstained soldier's uniform and, leaning against a prop tree, transformed herself into the wounded young man of her patriotic *Aux Champs d'Honneur*. No local reaction to her performance was published—though it remained a vivid memory for those who were fortunate enough to be at the Harris that night. There is a suspicion that far fewer people turned out than had greeted her the night before in Charlotte's sold-out Academy of Music, since tickets were still available until curtain time.

As the Harris continued to offer both the exceptional and the tried-and-true, its management faced a new

HARRIS THEATRE, TUESDAY NIGHT, JAN. 9

Last Appearance of the World's Greatest Artiste

MME. SARAH

BERNHARDT

With Her Complete Company and Productions from the
Theatre Sarah Bernhardt, Paris

in

"CLEOPATRA"
"CAMILLE"
"CHAMPS D'HONNEUR"
"THE HUSBAND'S LUCK"
BERNHARDT IN FOUR FAMOUS ROLES
SEATS NOW ON SALE

Caution:—Patrons please come early, as no one will be admitted after curtain rises. Plenty of good seats left.

PRICES: $2.50, $2.00, $1.50, $1.00.

problem: by 1915, the number of touring companies cast in New York had dropped fifty percent from its peak at the beginning of the century. Now it was becoming increasingly difficult to avoid dark nights at the theatre. The theatre season at the Harris normally ran from September through May. Summer heat made most of America's theatres virtually unusable for several months, since cooling systems consisted only of fans that drew out stale air, and both men and women still wore layers of clothing that contributed to the discomfort. There were, of course, many warm weather entertainments, ranging from outdoor ballgames to tent shows and amusement parks. Baseball was popular in Spartanburg, and the sport drew a wide range of spectators. Social segregation was in effect even in the ballpark, and Spartans did not always mingle freely. An item in *The Herald* on July 25, 1907, reported that two women from a "disreputable part of town" had been arrested for going to a ballgame and sitting with "ladies." To add to the indignity, the names of the two women detained were given, even though they had not committed a crime.

The Movies Come to Town

*O*nly a year or two before the opening of the Harris, the first small movie theatres or nickelodeons, the Magic and the Fairyland, had opened just off Morgan Square on Magnolia Street, and were soon joined by the Electric on Kennedy Place. Programs of ten-minute one-reelers were soon drawing in a steady stream of fascinated Spartans, and the operators could repeat the short programs from 2:30 p.m. until 11 p.m. By 1909, movies were growing longer, films that told a story were becoming available, and the showing of films with a live program of vaudeville performers became the rule. Since most of the early nickelodeons had no stage facilities, somewhat larger theatres with performance areas were now being built around the United States. Through newspaper ads, the public was asked to suggest

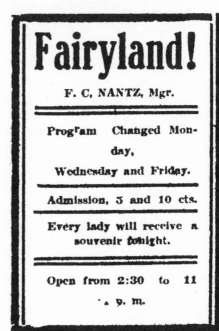

Fairyland!

F. C. NANTZ, Mgr.

Program Changed Monday,

Wednesday and Friday.

Admission, 5 and 10 cts.

Every lady will receive a souvenir tonight.

Open from 2:30 to 11

p. m.

names for a new movie-vaudeville house scheduled to open in Spartanburg at 145 North Church Street—only a short distance south of the Harris; and when it did open in the winter of 1909, it was called the Royal Palace. It offered both films and vaudeville acts, and manager W. E. Baker advertised "Three Gilden Sisters (Broadway Swells)," singing, bone solos, novelty tricks, and clog dancing at a single matinee and two evening performances, for the modest admission price of ten cents (children, five cents). At the Harris, a more sophisticated evening of vaudeville would cost fifty cents for orchestra seats and fifteen cents for the second balcony (or gallery).

In no time, another theatre in the same area opened at 156 North Church, across the street from the Harris. Simply called the Royal, it advertised vaudeville and films for a dime. Perhaps the Royal had simply replaced the Royal Palace, but both soon closed. All the major theatres of future years, with the notable exception of the Montgomery, would be located in the long block of East Main between Church and Liberty streets. The first of the Main Street theatres, the Lyric, opened in April 1909, at number 136 (later renumbered 140). Like its predecessors on North Church, it combined movies with live entertainment until the sound era when it became the Criterion. Actually, the Lyric seated slightly more than 300 persons, but it was advertised as "a cool place" and "Spartanburg's most up-to-date theatre." The long, narrow, and steeply-raked auditorium offered a décor that featured the

AT THE

Royal Palace

ALL THIS WEEK

Three
GILDEN SISTERS

Broadway Swells

ONE OF THE BIGGEST ACTS
EVER PRESENTED HERE.

Introducing Singing, Bone Solos,
Talking and Champion Novelty Trick
Clog Dancing; giving a complete
change of program on Thursday.

Only One Matinee In the Afternoon, Beginning at 4:30.

Admission, 10c.
Children 5c in afternoon.

W. E. BAKER, MGR.
145 North Church Street.

masks of comedy and tragedy on its side panels and over the small proscenium. At first, white tile walled the entrance, but a later application of plaster and gilt gave it a warmer appearance. It would operate over thirty years under a variety of names (Tivoli, Majestic, Rialto, Omar) and under managements that were often short-lived. For several years, it was called the Rex, which was changed when the much larger "new" Rex was built on the opposite side of East Main.

The move to Main Street accelerated the following year (1910) when Lawrence Lester, Jr., proprietor of the Magic and Fairyland "electric" theatres on Magnolia Street, opened his Grand Theatre across the street from the Lyric. Lester's own photograph was featured in many of his advertisements, and he proclaimed his new theatre "the house beautiful"—a term used frequently at the time to describe new theatres. The exact seating capacity of the Grand is unknown, but Lester's claim that it was twice as big as any other movie theatre in town was probably hyperbole, since the fairly reliable Julius Cahn-Gus Hill national directory of theatres listed it as only a 346-seat house a decade later. Located at 139 East Main, it occupied half of the property that would become McClellan's Five and Ten in 1924, and the theatre's most distinguishing exterior feature was a pair of bulb-studded crescent signs on either side of the entrance. Its stage facilities were at least large enough to accommodate the vaudeville and specialty acts that were regularly booked, and it was equipped with a photoplayer to accompany silent films. Photoplayers were actually small pipe organs that were installed just under the stage and were operated from a piano-like console. What made them especially attractive to theatre owners was their ability to play automatically with long rolls similar to those used on a player piano. A professional musician was not required to operate the photoplayer, and often an usher or doorman would be in charge of changing music rolls and controlling the instrument.

One Good Week Deserves Another

In view of this fact, I have decided to keep

THE

Howze Sisters

For another week. They will introduce new songs and dances each and every day. I have for Monday

4 Swell Reels

Big Feature Vitagraph next Tuesday,

"THE MYSTERY OF SILVESKULL," Featuring Maurice Costello.

At The

GRAND

Of Course!

Although Lawrence Lester obviously took great pride in his new theatre, it did not prove to be his ultimate dream house. In 1913 he built the Lester (later renamed the Strand) just east of the Lyric, and his instincts about the importance of theatre magic for audiences were so well served in the design of this lovely showplace that it remained one of Spartanburg's most durable and popular places of entertainment for more than three decades. All of the amenities of the 800-seat auditorium—modern heating and ventilation, fire exits, wide aisles, and "seats of comfort" were spelled out in the large ads he placed in local newspapers. He added the final touch by installing a Möller theatre organ (Opus 1723) at a cost of $2,000. For the opening night, Lester almost outdid the glamorous opening evening at the Harris. He announced that the first 1,000 patrons would receive a red carnation. In a conservative town like Spartanburg, this gesture no doubt had some practical value, especially in making the theatre "respectable" for women to attend. The Lester's small stage and limited backstage facilities were inadequate for elaborate touring operettas and plays, but they served nicely for the popular musical routines, novelty acts, and short skits that had become popular. As part of the opening night program, the Lester

---

Lawrence Lester frequently used his own photograph in his theatres' newspaper ads.

also boasted a small orchestra under the direction of Lynwood Maxwell Williamson at the piano (Williamson would later become musical director at the Rex). The other musicians were Marie Epton (violin), Harry Hardy (trombone), Sam Cantrell (cornet), and Frank Saffomani (drums). The orchestra would play on other occasions, too, but more often, the Möller organ accompanied the film showings.

The large Harris Theatre had set a pattern of designating sections of the house for black patrons, at least for certain attractions, but the new movie-vaudeville theatres on Main Street offered no such admissions. Lawrence Lester was quite aware of the potential audience among African-Americans, and the same year that he built his namesake theatre, he opened the Globe, the first "colored" theatre in town, near the end of a block of black businesses on South Liberty Street at number 190. Since no ads for the Globe ran in the principal newspapers, there is no record of the featured films (and possibly live performances).

In other nearby cities, someone had to take the initiative in bringing the movies to town, but none could have been more colorful than Lawrence Lester. The photograph that accompanied a number of his ads while he was the impresario of Main Street suggests that he was pudgy and still rather young. In his memories of

About Accomodations of •

THE

LESTER

This house is the last word in Moving Picture Palaces—as near perfect as perfect can be—no time nor money has been spared in making it all that you would have it be. We have installed—

The Latest Hot Air Heating Apparatus.
Best and Latest System of Ventilation.
Indirect Lighting system.
Two Large Fire Exits in the Rear.
Moving Picture Machines of the Latest Type.
Incline Floor, Wide Aisles, "Seats of Comfort."

1000 Beautiful Carnations Free Tomorrow

—THE—

LESTER

"Spartanburg's Theatre Beautiful"

Spartanburg, Joseph M. McLaughlin described him as "a whopping big fellow weighing about 250," and aptly compared him to silent film comedian Fatty Arbuckle. He also noted that Lester walked like Charlie Chaplin—not from imitation but because he had flat feet and "rheumatism." Since he lived in the one hundred block of North Converse Street, he did not have to spend too much time on his feet to walk between home and his theatres. Lester's other recorded passion besides motion pictures was playing pool, which he did expertly at a pool hall not far from the Lester Theatre. But his reign was to be short; for by 1915 both of his Main Street theatres had been sold to separate companies and his Magnolia Street nickelodeons were no longer operating.

It is strange that a person so involved in the entertainment business would divest himself of all his holdings at a time when movies were growing in popularity and profitability. There are hints of some of his problems in the newspaper ads. In one for the Grand in 1913 he announced: "There won't be singing for the rest of the week; there was a misunderstanding with the booking agent; he sent a vaudeville act instead of moving picture entertainers, so I wouldn't use them but one day." This suggests that Lawrence Lester was not a very sophisticated man and that as an independent showman he was having difficulty obtaining shows and acts that he considered suitable. He lived on the same street (North Converse) as the Greenewald brothers, but he may never have exchanged ideas about the state of the theatrical world with them. The large Harris Theatre booked its musicals, plays, and variety shows through the controlling syndicates in New York and frequently advertised "Keith" vaudeville. Keith was a name associated with the best popular entertainers who went out on tour from America's theatre capital. Film distribution was also becoming tightly controlled, so that men like Lawrence Lester (if indeed there was another just like him) were being edged out. These also may have been the reasons for the failure of a small theatre called the Vandette, which operated briefly on Magnolia Street in 1912-13 with the standard movie-vaudeville program in fashion—or in this case it may simply have been an unpopular location or insufficient amenities for audiences accustomed to the comfort of the new theatres built by Lester.

The new operators of the Grand and the Lester renamed them the Bijou and the Strand respectively. For a while, the Lyric operated as the Rex, offering films accompanied by a small orchestra and a variety of singers, dancers, acrobats, and comics. In 1917, a larger "new" Rex was built by C. H. Henry on the south side of East Main, on the site of a former livery stable, and the Lyric was rechristened (yet again) as the Rialto. Spartanburg had acquired a new,

beautifully designed and appointed theatre. The new Rex had a spacious outer lobby, elegant seats backed with burgundy and gold cut velvet in the orchestra and large balcony, and a striking proscenium hung with satin and velvet. Although its stage and backstage facilities were designed with only vaudeville entertainment in mind, they were considerably larger than those of the other three motion picture houses on Main Street. In ambiance and amenities, it was the

The entrance of the Bijou Theatre on East Main Street before 1920.
—*Courtesy, Martin Meek*

Most of the major silent films were shown at the Rex. This photo from the 1920s shows the console of the Wurlitzer organ, left, and the piano-like console of a Photoplayer, center. —*Courtesy, Wofford College*

closest thing to a movie palace that Spartans would see for a number of years.

Lawrence Lester, Jr. had opened his second "house beautiful" the year that Woodrow Wilson was elected president of the United States; Europe would erupt into war the next year, the *Herald* would give headlines to the sinking of the Lusitania in 1915, and Spartanburg would soon feel the effects of World War I, both socially and economically. For some it would offer new experiences, opportunities, and exposure to new ideas; for others it would bring personal grief and irreparable loss.

~*3*~

The Effects of the War Years

orld War I brought new audiences to the existing theatres in town, as more than 20,000 trainees at Camp Wadsworth sought entertainment and escape—as well as a hot shower at the prospering Atlantic bathhouse on Magnolia Street. Located only a few miles to the west of the city, the army camp had its own Picto theatre; inadequately heated by coal stoves in winter, it was no match for the more inviting show places in Spartanburg. Several new theatres sprang up to meet the demand: the Bonita on West Main, opposite the Cleveland Hotel, and two "colored" theatres, the Star and the Atlas, on North Church. The latter two came into existence to provide an entertainment choice for several thousand black trainees denied admission to the Main Street houses. Except for two periods, when the theatres were closed because of a meningitis threat and for the deadly flu epidemic of 1918, the bulb-studded theatre signs flashed on East Main, West Main, and North Church streets, and lines formed at the box offices on weekends.

The billings make evident the popularity of vaudeville. A typical show at the Strand was "Fads and Follies," described as "clean, clever, and classy," and featuring Chas. Brewer ("Comedian"), Williams and Ray ("Buck

STRAND

ALL WEEK

CHAS. BREWERS

Fads and Follies

Musical Comedy Company in a Repertoire of

CLEAN, CLEVER AND CLASSY

Tabloid Musical Comedies

The Best Show ever Offered at

POPULAR PRICES

Featuring

CHAS. BREWER

Comedian

WILLIAMS and RAY

Buck Dancers

And a Bevy of Bright, Beautiful and Bewitching

Fair Damsels Who Can

SING AND DANCE

Change of Program

Monday, Wednesday and Friday

STRAND THEATRE

Dancers"), plus "a bevy of Bright, Beautiful and Bewitching Fair Damsels Who Can SING AND DANCE." Whether the alliteration that pervaded the ad was a creation of the company's producer or the theatre manager's own inspiration, it was calculated to lure young recruits to the box office. A bill advertised at the Harris, which booked only the class acts of the New York-based Keith circuit, starred Lou Holtz and featured "Yankee and Dixie, the Comedy Dogs," "Armstrong & Strouse, lively, singing and dancing couple," "The Dooleys, the Eastern Girl and the Western Boy," and "Newkirk and Homer Girls, an up-to-date Song and Dance Review"—all this for 15-25 cents at the matinee and 25-50 cents, plus war tax, at the evening performance. Even the short-lived Bonita on Morgan Square competed with such attractions as "Chief Wongo Nemah and Princess Floating Cloud in Oklahoma Indian songs and dances" (in addition to short films).

Far more elaborate plays and musicals of all varieties continued on the large stage of the Harris, and of special interest in 1918 were the all-soldier musicals—from Camp Wadsworth the New York 27th Regiment's *You Know Me Al!* in March, and on November 14, 1918 (three days after the signing of the Armistice) Camp Jackson's *As You Were*. Some of the creators in *You Know Me Al!* either had previous professional theatre credits before entering the U.S. Army or would go on after the war to careers on Broadway. Hugh Stanislaus Stange, the coauthor of the book, had even written the libretto for an operetta by De Koven, the composer whose *The Red Feather* had opened the Harris a decade earlier. Harry (Wagstaff) Gribble, the show's director, would later write numerous plays and direct such Broadway successes as *Johnny Belinda* and *Anna Lucasta*. The show itself was a musical farce in a style already familiar to theatregoers at the Harris. The plot was light and no doubt predictable, but it served as a frame-work for some eighteen musical numbers. These included an obligatory salute to the armed forces, "My Heart Belongs to the U.S.A.," for the leading man and chorus, a torch song called "I'm Old Enough for a Little Loving," and a love duet for leading man and the soldier playing the leading lady, "Let Me Have a Corner of Your Heart." As a photograph of the company proves, the drag component was strong on authenticity, with stylish costumes and credible makeup. Since it was all done for "fun," Arline, Sally, and the "female" chorus did not trouble the many Spartans and soldiers from Camp Wadsworth who saw the show. Two of the supporting roles, Lotta Noyes and Knotta Sounde, have an oddly contemporary resonance. The show had its dress rehearsal on the Harris stage and played the week of March 25, 1918, before delighted audiences.

Of course, home entertainments of a sort had already reached Spartanburg by World War I. The parlor organ had given way to the player piano, on which all the latest songs could be played automatically with piano rolls, and almost everyone in town (or in the county) seemed to have a victrola or gramophone, which could be purchased for as little as $12 or as much as an astronomical $900. The top recording stars were not only popular vaudeville per-formers but also opera singers who were the original "crossover" artists in the early years of the phonograph. In 1918, Spartans could purchase Geraldine Farrar's "The War Baby's Lullaby" or Enrico Caruso's recording of the top wartime hit, "Over There." The latter, a ten-inch 78 rpm, had the steep price of two dollars, which was more than the cost of a ticket for the best seat at the Harris. It is little wonder that live entertainment remained a potent draw for all levels of society, even with the competition of the

This memorable sketch of the dress rehearsal of the all-soldier show *You Know Me Al* in 1918 suggests the size of the Harris Theatre's large stage, while providing glimpses of a male chorus line, a victrola used as a prop, and the elaborate scenery being set up. —*Courtesy, Spartanburg Regional Museum*

movies.

There were more than a few stage-struck young Spartans who wanted to go a step further than buying a ticket: they wanted to go onstage, at a time when most of their parents viewed actors as socially unacceptable. Still, local people had sometimes worked as extras or pit musicians since the days of the Opera House, when a touring company needed to supplement the bodies onstage or fill out an operetta orchestra. After the opening of the Harris, the need had increased. In that pivotal year of 1918, a group of prominent young women dared criticism to star in an amateur musical at the Harris. Called *Fru-Fru*, it offered songs, skits, and a fashion revue, with one scene set in the Astor Hotel roof garden. At the sold-out performance on August 17, "the talented Miss Grace Dupre scored in her dance and whistling number," and Mrs. Walter Montgomery, Mrs. E. S. Tennent, and Miss Rosa Black all demonstrated some thespian talents. A year earlier, local talent, including Mrs. Montgomery, had had another outing by appearing in a feature silent film called *The Wrecker*, which filled the Rex Theatre with audiences intensely curious to see people they knew perform on screen to the accompaniment of Lynwood Maxwell Williamson's small orchestra.

As feature films were becoming the main attraction, the Main Street theatres were in the process of upgrading their facilities. In November, the Bijou announced the installation of a new photoplayer, which was "similar but larger than the one in the Rialto." The Strand did even better by reportedly adding a new theatre organ at a reported cost of $10,000. Why the older Möller organ needed replacement is unclear; it is possible that the new organ was actually a very sophisticated new photoplayer that relieved the theatre management of maintaining a full-time staff of organists.

~*4*~

The Roaring (sometimes) Twenties

*C*hanges occurred in rapid succession after the signing of the Armistice in November 1918. Camp Wadsworth closed and the remaining trainees boarded trains for their hometowns, leaving Spartanburg's stores and theatres with far fewer customers. The Eighteenth Amendment to the Constitution, prohibiting the sale of alcoholic beverages and their importation, was ratified in 1919; the following year the momentous Nineteenth Amendment allowed women to vote for the first time. That same year the theatre scene in Spartanburg changed dramatically: the Harris was condemned as a playhouse and the theatre section of the building was scheduled for demolition. According to reports, the inferior brick used in the construction of the walls had begun to deteriorate, and repairs were either too costly or

Montgomery Theatre

FRIDAY NIGHT, DECEMBER 16

Hear them sing "HALLELUJAH"

VINCENT YOUMANS

Hear them sing "SOMETIMES I'M HAPPY"

presents
THE NAUTICAL MUSICAL COMEDY SUCCESS

HIT THE DECK

Book by HERBERT FIELDS

Music by VINCENT YOUMANS

lines by LEO ROBIN and CLIFFORD GREY

with MARION SAKI

a capable cast of stars and a large singing, dancing chorus

company of 60

SPECIAL AUGMENTED ORCHESTRA

NOW THE RAGE OF NEW YORK and CHICAGO

MAIL ORDERS NOW.   SEAT SALE THURSDAY

Prices including tax: Orchestra $3.60, $3.00.
Balcony $2.40, $1.80, $1.20.

even impossible. The theatre no doubt had other drawbacks. After more than a dozen years of constant use, it was in need of total refurbishing; it also needed an efficient cooling system to make it usable year-round. Perhaps even more of a problem was its design, with steep, curving balconies that may have made it unsuitable for conversion to films. By now, Isaac Greenewald had left his post at the Harris, and in its final season (1919-20), under the management of J. R. Harris, Jr., the theatre offered local audiences their last opportunity to see a major professional musical for some five years. It was Arthur Hammerstein's production of *Sometime*, by Rudolph Friml and Rida Johnson Young, leading contributors to the Broadway stage throughout the 1920s. Many of the last bookings were lightweight comedies, such as *Up in Mabel's Room*, *Bringing up Father in Society*, and *Mutt and Jeff's Dream*.

The office and shop sections of the Harris Building remained virtually unchanged, but the theatre's stage housing section had simply disappeared. For a while, the lights dimmed on North Church Street, and the businesses that had profited from their proximity to the playhouse were deprived of customers. What went unreported was the impact of the theatre's closing on individuals: theatre staff, cleaning crew, as well as the electrician and stagehands who had made the performances possible found themselves unemployed. In October 1921, when the theatre season normally began, the John B. Williams Stock Company offered a week of plays in a tent set up on Magnolia Street. It proved so popular that a heating system of sorts was installed, and the group was held over for a second week. It confirmed that there was still an eager audience for live performances in town, but it was only a temporary and unsatisfactory substitute.

For the movie theatres, it was the beginning of the final and most glorious decade of silent films. The Rex and the Strand both boasted theatre organs or photoplayers that made seeing the silents so memorable. In addition to the organists and projectionists, they employed a full staff of ushers. Just as in cities large and small across America, Spartans never said, "I'm going to the movies." Rather they specified, "I'm going to the Rex," "I'm going to the Strand." Those names defined the experience as much as did the film shown, and there were social implications in one's choice of theatre. The Rialto was considered déclassé and many ladies in town would never consider attending a theatre with "girlie" shows. However, the comic vaudevillians and chorus girls may have been risqué only by the most conservative standards. Some Spartans never set foot in any of the theatres, and in the churches of the more conservative denominations ministers were known to condemn all moviegoing as sinful. When Cecil B. DeMille's *The Ten Commandments* ran in 1923, audiences discovered that it wasn't all about Moses, even though the parting of the Red Sea was excitingly depicted in two-strip Technicolor. Much of the film was devoted to a series of contemporary stories about people who broke those Ten Commandments.

But no entertainments could have been less corrupting than the popular comedies of Charlie Chaplin, Harold Lloyd, and Buster Keaton, which returned repeatedly to local screens. Lon Chaney was frightening to perfection in *The Phantom of the Opera* and *The Unholy Three*, and deeply moving in his clown role in *He Who Gets Slapped*. Mary Pickford charmed even the cynical in one saccharine film after another, while Gloria Swanson personified the daring woman. *The Four Horsemen of the Apocalypse, Blood and Sand*, and *The Sheik* featured a new kind of male sexuality in the person of Rudolph Valentino, and the director, Rex Ingram, who had made Valentino a star, did the same in 1924 for a young Mexican named Ramon Novarro in *Scaramouche*.

By now, the movie theatres had become a haven for a varied public from all elements and levels of society. They provided a place where young people could bring their dates and even venture some physical contact. And some clandestine lovers hoped to go unrecognized in the dim light of the balcony. After school, teenagers flocked to the matinees, and lonely people found some reprieve from their loneliness. As across America and much of the world, movies had become a craze, and the actors who performed in them set tastes and suggested possibilities unrealizable in Spartanburg. The Sunday edition of the local paper now featured a full theatre page, and many fans of all ages turned to it before reading the comics, the society pages, or the local and world news. It contained ads for all the theatres, scenes from upcoming films or stage shows, and a complete listing of the film programs for the week. Some teenagers were so fascinated by the movies that they clipped the ads of the films they saw to paste in scrapbooks, often along with their ticket stubs.

The most important change in the face of downtown in the 1920s was the construction of the Montgomery building on the northeast corner of North Church and St. John (Elm) streets. A new and richly decorated theatre would be an integral part of this impressive ten-story office structure, and it would be located on the site of the

The stage, orchestra pit and front areas of the Montgomery Theatre as it looked in 1925. —*Courtesy, Lockwood Greene*

turreted Montgomery mansion where years before the Montgomery children had no doubt watched from their upstairs rooms as the crowds arrived at the Harris Theatre directly across the street. With more than 1,300 seats, the new Montgomery would be the largest theatre in town and one of the finest in the Southeast. The types of interior materials used in the construction gave it a luxury unapproached in any earlier theatres in Spartanburg, and it would become the city's pride when it provided a stage for large touring companies once again, after an absence of almost five years. At about the same time as the opening of the Montgomery, a new "colored" theatre named the Dunbar opened just a shout away on a narrow side street that ran between North Church and Magnolia. It was no larger than the Lyric but had an attractive arched front studded with light bulbs. On Short Wofford Street, there was a nucleus of black restaurants, businesses and, of course, the theatre—but many white Spartans passed their entire lives without ever venturing that shortcut to the Court House. The unintimidated who did were far wiser about the social and racial fabric of their city.

The Montgomery provided the ultimate magic for the theatregoer for decades. At first there was no exterior box office, and patrons walked up a slightly elevated, vaulted arcade under a series of chandeliers to a box office built into the marble wall, near the triple pairs of curtained French doors that marked the entrance into the elegant inner lobby. Entering the theatre through a second, more widely spaced trio of French doors, patrons first glimpsed the beautiful stained-glass soffit fixtures under the balcony; and then beyond the balcony six clustered chandeliers with gleaming baskets of crystal pendants set in a gilded frame above the auditorium. The wood-paneled lower area of the walls no doubt contributed to the superb acoustics. Gilded Grecian motifs decorated the wide and tall proscenium, framed by two levels of stage boxes—the lower ones functional and the upper ones designed to conceal the theatre organ pipes (never to be installed, as it turned out).

Unlike many theatres that booked both stage entertainments and films, the Montgomery provided an excellent environment for both. Although the orchestra was five or six rows deeper than a typical Broadway playhouse, a sense of intimacy with the stage was maintained, and Spartans saw plays, musicals, and vaudeville acts very much as their counterparts in larger cities. For film viewing, there were few seats that did not afford an unobstructed and undistorted view of the screen. And of no small significance was the modern cooling system that the theatre boasted.

For all the excitement surrounding the opening of the new showplace, the curtain went up for the first time with little fanfare. The first performance on the stage, on October 16, 1925, was a matinee of Al C. Field's Minstrels, followed by an evening performance at 8 p.m. The minstrel show in blackface had long been a staple of popular entertainment in the United States, but it seemed an odd choice for the inauguration of a theatre in 1925. It may simply have reflected the tastes of the first independent lessees of the house, Mr. and Mrs. J. R. Pattie, who had arrived in town from another small city (Frankfort, Kentucky). In any case, subsequent bookings included new operettas, sophisticated musicals, plays, and vaudeville

GRAND OPENING
MONTGOMERY THEATER

FRI., OCT. 16

Matinee—Night

A.L.C.
FIELD
MINSTRELS

OLDEST
AND BEST

Jack Richards, Bert Swor, Billy Church, Harry Frankel, John
Healy, Joe McGee and fifty minstrel favorites.
Prices Plus Tax—Night...................$2.00, $1.50, $1.00, 50c
Matinee...................$1.50, $1.00, 75c, 50c
Seats on Sale MONDAY—Martin's Drug Store
Phone 2283 for Tickets

that recalled the finest days of the Harris. From 1926 until 1928, Spartanburg enjoyed a short-lived theatrical renaissance, but the years between 1925 and 1929 would be the last time that Spartans would have full seasons of professional theatre. In fact, the stage was so fully booked that only a handful of silent films were ever shown on the screen, and they were lesser Hollywood productions, with accompaniment by a small orchestra or simply a piano. That first fall season at the Montgomery brought a variety of entertainment to the stage. If a minstrel show seemed a bit passé to some, then ten days later there was the most sophisticated musical that Broadway had to offer: George and Ira Gershwin's *Lady be Good*; and for the spectacle-minded, *George White's Scandals* ("with augmented orchestra and three cars of gorgeous effects"). In December, the theatre (now under the management of Aro Amusements, Inc.) even gave local audiences a taste of Shakespeare, when the company of veteran tourer Robert B. Mantell performed *Julius Caesar* and *Macbeth*.

In less than a year, the original lessees had departed and the Montgomery had become a part of the growing Paramount-Publix chain of theatres that already operated the Rex and Strand; E.E. Whitaker had been appointed the theatre's manager. The 1926-27 season brought the Rudolph Friml operetta *Rose Marie*, with a company of seventy and Romberg's *The Student Prince* (with only sixty) as well as numerous revues, vaudeville acts, and straight plays. While local audiences were not being introduced to Ibsen or Shaw, they did get Somerset Maugham's deliciously amoral comedy *The Constant Wife*, in which the perceptive critic might detect undertones of *A Doll's House*. At least part of the attraction of the touring version of this recent Broadway success was the presence of the fading silent film star and notorious consort of the famous, Lou Tellegan, who was conveniently cast in a role in which his persistent Dutch accent did not seem inappropriate. Tellegan's acting talents were modest at best, but he had been the companion of the much older Sarah Bernhardt and then had married the celebrated opera diva Geraldine Farrar. That was enough to sell more than a few tickets to the Montgomery in 1927. Tellegan's co-stars, Charlotte Walker and Norman Hackett, were respected veterans of Broadway and touring, and only a few months before had played the Montgomery stage in another sophisticated play, Michael Arlen's *The Green Hat.*

In September 1926, both Vitaphone and Movietone sound equipment were installed, making the Montgomery one of the first theatres in the Southeast to show the early sound shorts being released by Warner Brothers and the first talking newsreels. In 1927, Warners released dozens of the mainly one-reel shorts, shown very much as a segment of a vaudeville evening. Since most featured leading artists of opera, stage, and vaudeville who were unlikely to appear live, they afforded an opportunity to both see and hear a variety of acclaimed performers. The Vitaphone shorts included popular music by Fred Waring and His Pennsylvanians, gospel music by the Utica Jubilee Singers, and operatic excerpts by Gigli, De Luca, and other Metropolitan Opera singers. Mme. Ernestine Schumann Heink sang "Danny Boy" and varied songs in her ten-minute stint. The famous German contralto, already familiar to many through her recordings, would enjoy popularity as a radio performer well into her seventies. These performances, however, usually filmed head-on with a single camera and little physical movement, remained curiosities, and the sound film did not make significant inroads for the next two years.

Feature films remained silent, and the Rex continued to be the prime showcase for them in Spartanburg. In 1927, Publix was so convinced that silents would endure that they installed a splendid new Wurlitzer organ in the Rex and an expensive Wurlitzer Photoplayer at the Strand. Some of the major films of the period, such as *Ben Hur* and *The Big Parade*, played the Rex with a touring orchestra of some twenty musicians that accompanied the prints of the films. Exactly two years after the installation of

Vitaphone in the Montgomery, *The Jazz Singer* opened for a momentous week's run, and from that date on the Montgomery was the leading first-run motion picture theatre in Spartanburg, even as it continued to book plays, musicals, and vaudeville. Meanwhile, the old Rialto attempted a comeback under a new management that renamed it the Omar and spent some $3,000 to improve the stage facilities and add seats. But the age of cut-rate vaudeville was drawing to a close, and talking pictures would soon became the rage; in a few years, the stage facilities in Spartanburg's smallest theatre were simply eliminated.

The year 1929 brought a feast of new talkie musicals, some of them versions of the same operettas and musicals that Spartans had just seen on the stage at the Montgomery. More often than not, it would be a new musical created just for the screen that left the most enduring impression. Al Jolson's second part-talkie, *The Singing Fool*, had audiences wiping their eyes and rushing to the record counters to buy the Brunswick ten-inch recording of "Sonny Boy," with "There's a Rainbow 'Round my Shoulder," which people would whistle while walking down the street. The two-strip Technicolor *Gold Diggers of Broadway* offered another, even more whistleable melody, "Tiptoe Through the Tulips," and the Nick Lucas recording of the song was big seller in town. The days of Tiny Tim's squeaky rendition of that tune were decades in the future. Another enduring number, "Singin' in the Rain," had its first outing in the all-star *Hollywood Revue of 1929*, and the sheet music's cover for the hit song featured all of the MGM galaxy. There was also music in the air quite literally: Spartans were beginning to buy radios, and with an antenna, the voices of many of the same singers could be heard live from distant stations in Cincinnati, Chicago, or New York.

In the spring of that year, the *Herald* reported that both the Strand and the Rex would also be wired for sound films, but only the Strand was actually converted. The Rex closed its doors on June 1 after the final evening showing of *The Pagan*, starring Ramon Novarro. MGM had also released a version with recorded music sound effects and a song sung by Novarro; Spartans got the all-silent release, and it was no competition for the talkies at the Montgomery even with a major star like Novarro in semi-undress. The Strand announced a "Gala Opening of TALKING, SINGING-PICTURES" for June 21 with a now-forgotten film called *Prisoners* (the first talkie outing for the popular and photogenic Corinne Griffith). With the closing of the Rex, the almost-new Wurlitzer organ would be heard no more as vibrant accompaniment to a silent feature or mirthful underscoring for a cartoon. The silent era had ended, and the theatre organ at the Rex and the new Wurlitzer Photoplayer at the Strand were excess baggage.

~5~

The Depression Years

Although no one suspected it in 1929, the stock market crash in the fall of that year and the Depression years that would follow put an end to the construction of new theatres in Spartanburg for more than a decade. It would also have a dramatic impact on the entertainment that was available. No longer would there be touring musicals and plays on a regular basis, and a new generation would have few opportunities to experience what had been a vibrant part of the city's entertainment and social life for so many years. Vaudeville did continue on an almost weekly basis at the Montgomery, at least until the late 1930s, but fully staged plays or musicals became infrequent. For a while, in the darkest years of the Depression, only two theatres —the Montgomery and the Strand—were operating. The difference between the 25-cent admission at the Montgomery and the 15-cent admission at the Strand dictated where many people saw a film in those difficult years. After the prolonged closing of the Rex in June of 1929, the Montgomery had announced a new film policy: instead of two films a week, the theatre would show three. Audiences had obviously dwindled. The operetta craze that had begun with the introduction of sound ended abruptly, and the beautiful Technicolor Hammerstein-Romberg *Viennese Nights* had only a midweek run in 1931, even with the presence of the major Broadway musical star Vivienne Segal.

In 1932, the national Paramount-Publix theatre chain that operated the two houses was on the verge of bankruptcy, and both theatres were taken over by a North Carolina subsidiary of Publix, Wilby-Kincey. The Montgomery, rechristened "The Carolina," now shared the name that already adorned the marquees of the company's leading theatres in Winston-Salem, Greensboro, Charlotte, and Greenville. It was the period known as "pre-code," when films were able to deal realistically with themes and situations that would become censurable after 1934. Fallen or rebellious women abounded—portrayed by Ruth Chatterton, Nancy Carroll, Tallulah Bankhead, Kay Francis, Barbara Stanwyck, Norma Shearer, and other major stars of the period, in films with titles such as *Wayward*, *Possessed*, *Anybody's Woman*, and *Faithless*. Warner Brothers caught the public's attention with a series of hard-hitting crime films, and Paul Muni and Jimmy Cagney achieved stardom in them. Then Mae West arrived on the scene, and with her early pre-code films she brought Paramount back from bankruptcy. There were "women's films" and "men's films"—or at least they were perceived that way—and there were others, like those starring Will Rogers, that seemed to appeal to everyone. A few in the audience may even have remembered seeing Rogers himself on the Montgomery stage during that brief flourishing of live theatre in 1926-29, and by now just about everyone had heard his voice on radio.

In 1934, the Hollywood studios were abruptly forced to adhere to the Production Code that contained a series of prohibitions bordering on the ridiculous. Double beds suddenly became taboo, and if one believed the Hollywood version, all middle-class married couples slept in twin beds with a night table and lamp in between. Any deviation from the most conventional social behavior must be punished severely before the final "The End" hit the screen. In the 1930 tearjerker *Sarah and Son*, which won Ruth Chatterton an Oscar nomination for best actress that year, child star Philippe De Lacey shows contempt for his foster parents with a petulant "darn." When the mother rebukes him, he adds: " I wanted to say damn." At a 2003 showing of the film, the line got a good laugh; in all probability, the reaction was the same in 1930 at the Montgomery. Yet four years later, that mild four-letter word was strictly forbidden in any dialogue, much less that of a ten-year-old. Until 1939, no studio challenged the rule, but when David Selznick refused to remove "damn" from Clark Gable's exit line in *Gone with the Wind*, it became a *cause célèbre*. Hollywood did outwit the code enforcers from time to time with its own encoded messages—though not everyone in Spartanburg (or across America) got the point. Even the exhibitors became skittish about the possibility of offending local sensibilities, as if they were also both arbiters of taste and defenders of local morality.

The early years of Wilby-Kincey management established a pattern of two-day vaudeville runs at the Carolina, usually on Friday-Saturday dates. The bills were sometimes headed by a fading Hollywood star such as Betty Compson whose name still had resonance because of her earlier films. With titles like *Girls in Cellophane*, *Hollywood Revue*, and *Broadway Whirl*, there was no doubt a certain amount of recycling of material. Only occasionally did a major touring production reach Spartanburg now. The most historically important was the national company of Marc Connelly's *The Green Pastures*, in 1933, the all-black musical that featured among the older members of its cast some of the actors who had toured with and been nurtured by Sissieretta Jones, the Black Patti. However, the most memorable night of live theatre in the 1930s was the performance of *The Barretts of Wimpole Street* with an exceptional cast headed by Katharine

Cornell and Basil Rathbone.

Cornell was, of course, the most acclaimed American actress of her time, and Elizabeth Barrett Browning had become her signature role. There were other fine actors in the large cast, including a young and slender Orson Welles, George MacCready, and Brenda Forbes in supporting roles. On the night of April 25, 1934, the Carolina was filled to capacity, and the audience remained mesmerized throughout the long performance (three and a half hours). An unsigned review appeared in the *Herald* the following day, and in the critic's opinion Cornell was flawless and utterly natural, and the play was perhaps the finest ever performed in the city. The final lines of the review comment on the problems of bringing first-class stage productions to the city: "Even with a packed house, there was little profit for the theater in the venture, but it was done for the accommodation of its patrons..." Those who could not afford the price of a ticket to the live performance of *The Barretts of Wimpole Street* had a chance

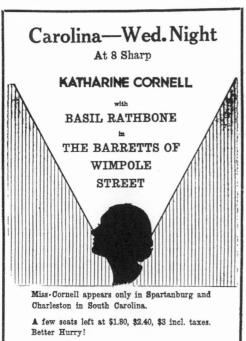

the same year to see Norma Shearer, Charles Laughton, and Fredric March on the Carolina's screen in MGM's superb (and enduring) film version of the play. Some would see it a second time at an even lower price when it returned to the Strand.

After being shuttered for some five years, the refurbished Rex reopened in 1934 as "The State." Under the management of the Palmetto Amusement Co. the theatre became the city's official "B" house—that is, it played programmers or "B" pictures that featured lesser actors and booked a weekly western, usually followed by a two-reel chapter of a serial film. Whereas the Rex had been decorated in warm colors, and its distinctive theatre seats featured panels of red and gold cut velvet, the remodeled house, with its new acoustical wall panels, was painted in shades of green, ranging from light to lugubrious. The heavy burgundy front curtain remained. Other changes were the addition of a marquee over the attractive brick archway at the entrance and the installation of a "washed air" cooling system.

Fortunately for moviegoers, the "new" State did not always limit its bookings to "B" films and westerns. From time to time, usually in the midweek Wednesday-Thursday slot, there were showings of re-releases of some unusual films from the beginning of the talkie era. These included *Frankenstein, Hell's Angels, All Quiet on the Western Front,* and the Norma Shearer tearjerker, *Smilin' Through.* The stage at the State also provided a place for local youngsters in Spartanburg to display their talents at the Saturday morning "Kiddee Klub." One of those eager performers was Dorothy Blackwell (Craig) who would later establish a dancing school where scores of children were trained. Wilby-Kincey also reopened the old Lyric as "The Criterion" in the mid-thirties and gave it an impressive marquee that seemed a bit grander than the theatre itself. The Strand resisted any major changes in its pleasing original design and continued as a reminder of Lawrence Lester's felicitous concept of "the house beautiful," even when its seats and carpet began to show the effects of long service. By 1934, three of the original four theatres on East Main were in business; only the Bijou had disappeared, its space incorporated into the new McClellan's Five and Ten in 1924.

A young native Mississippian named Robert Talbert had been designated both manager of the Carolina and "City Manager" when Wilby-Kincey assumed control of the local

An amused Robert Talbert, manager of the Carolina, placing scarce packs of cigarettes in the theatre's safe during World War II.
—*Courtesy, Mary Jane Sanders*

theatres. Short, dapper, and authoritative, he would remain at the helm for thirty-three years—in a company that normally transferred managers from city to city about as frequently as the Methodist Conference reassigned its ministers. Sometime managers of the other theatres were the Austell brothers (Dan and D.B.), Dave Garvin, Severn Allen, and Bill Nash. These exhibitors (as they preferred to be called) spent long hours devising ways to lure people into their theatres. Some films with popular stars were almost always profitable, but for others there were contests, drawings for prizes, "cooking schools" for women in the pre-matinee morning hours at the Carolina, local talent shows, and personal appearances by the likes of Roy Rogers and his horse Trigger. The large scene shop beneath the stage of the Carolina became an "art shop" where displays were designed and painted for all four theatres to promote their latest attractions. In addition to the usual one-sheets, banners, and stills provided by the film distributors, theatre entrances were often covered with locally-made displays liberally edged in glitter dust. Shadow boxes lit with bulbs and displaying one-sheets and stills stood along the walls of the theatre lobbies and in stairwells to announce coming attractions.

A great many 15-cent or 25-cent admissions were needed to stay in business, since film rentals, utilities, salaries for the staff ranging from projectionists to maintenance personnel had to be paid weekly. In addition, a percentage of the profits went to the local owners who had built the theatres as investments. In spite of the national economic crisis, the city's theatres continued to make a significant contribution to its economic life, even though attendance had declined. If touring actors registered far less frequently at local hotels, the theatres still brought large numbers of people downtown (or "uptown" as many Spartans preferred), and the lights still flashed enticingly in the evenings until the beginning of the final film showings around 9 p.m. In the difficult years of the Great Depression, when so many families across the nation were living in financial hardship, a weekly movie could be the only window to the world beyond and often gave hope for a happy ending.

Many moviegoers in the 1930s no doubt felt nostalgia for the days of exciting touring musicals that they had seen regularly on the stage of the Harris and, for a few brief years, at the Montgomery. Now Jeanette MacDonald and Nelson Eddy, onscreen in *Naughty Marietta* and *Sweethearts*, reminded them of those lilting Victor Herbert operettas from the past. From the mid-1930s on, younger audiences warmed to the popular dance musicals of Fred Astaire and Ginger Rogers, but they were growing up without experiencing the unique interaction between audience and live performers. At the same time, there were more than a few area residents who felt their entertainment needs fulfilled when they came to town on Saturdays and attended the first matinee of an "oater" at the State or Strand. It was even better if a western singing star made a guest appearance from time to time on stage.

In the 1930s, U.S. Highway 29 (then the main route between Washington and Atlanta) ran down Main Street in Spartanburg, just as it did in Greenville and many other small cities along the way. At the time there was some envy of Greenville's wider Main Street and its grid of cross streets, and city authorities were continually implementing plans to speed traffic through the city—often at the expense of its architecture and most distinctive landmarks. Streets that ended abruptly, such as Dunbar and St. John, were eventually extended and the buildings that stood in the way were demolished. Buses replaced the streetcars, and a bus station was created at the bandstand on the square. Only a wide cross-town boulevard might have alleviated the increasing congestion, leaving intact in the inner city the eclectic but interesting architectural mixture. As it was, the square underwent periodic and costly reconfigurations without improving the traffic flow appreciably.

Moviegoers in Spartanburg and across America came as close to film nirvana as they ever had in 1939-40. In 1939 alone, Hollywood studios released some of the most enduring (and enjoyable) films in motion picture history, and all of them played the Carolina, usually with a return engagement at the Strand a few months later. They included *The Wizard of Oz*, *Wuthering Heights*, *Ninotchka*, *The Women*, and *Gone with the Wind*, which would have a week's run early in 1940. When the dates for the showing of the Civil War epic were announced, anticipation increased. It was considered such an important event that students at Spartanburg High School were allowed to leave classes early to attend a matinee if they presented a written request from their parents. GWTW (as it came to be called) lived up to expectations, and it was presented at the Carolina with elements of calculated theatricality suggested by the distributors. After the overture of themes from the film score concluded, the houselights and footlights abruptly went out; there was an echoing drumroll as the velvet front curtain rapidly parted, followed by the parting of an inner sateen curtain, and the Selznick logo lit the darkened screen. At that moment, those now familiar, windblown titles swept across, accompanied by the equally familiar Tara theme. More than a few in the audience felt a tingle up their spines. It was a moment in moviegoing history never to be replicated.

In the spring of 1940, the old Criterion closed its doors for good with a showing of a Gene Autry western, and a new Main Street theatre, the Palmetto, was going up at the corner of East Main and North Liberty. The first news reports that Spartanburg was going to have its first new theatre in fifteen years suggested that it would be built somewhere between North Church and

Magnolia, but it was soon announced that it would replace some small business establishments in the prime location across the street from the Aug. W. Smith department store. The fairly small lot dictated the dimensions of the *art-moderne* structure, and the Palmetto ended up with a slightly larger seating capacity than the Strand only by providing a much larger balcony. This comfortable movie house was designed precisely for a current need—though it was a need that the Wilby-Kincey chain believed would continue indefinitely. There were no stage facilities at all, and the auditorium tapered down to a proscenium that was almost a perfect frame for films of the standard 1:1.33 aspect ratio. A curtain sparkling with glitter dust opened and closed automatically at the beginning and end of each feature film. The staggered seats were the most comfortable in town, and the red carpet with its abstract design the deepest. One innovation that brought delight to dating couples and inspired more than a few jokes was the half-dozen or so double seats, in which two people could sit comfortably without the obstacle of an armrest between them.

Under its first manager, James Cartledge, none of the amenities was slighted, even though many of its early offerings were "B" pictures of the Blondie, Sherlock Holmes, and Maisie variety. With uniformed doormen and a roster of six ushers, patrons were assured that their new theatre was a class act. Fortunately, for the real film connoisseur, the Palmetto also showed a number of unusual films not considered to be of sufficient box-office potential to play the Carolina. These included some pictures that are now established classics for one reason or another: *The Ox-Bow Incident, The Magnificent Ambersons, The Devil and Daniel Webster (All That Money Can Buy)*, Von Sternberg's campy *The Shanghai Gesture, Two-faced Woman* (Garbo's final film), and several of the pre-*Casablanca* films of Ingrid Bergman. Manager Cartledge was one film exhibitor who was an unabashed movie fan himself. In the early 1940s he was a familiar figure at the Carolina on

A Bob Hope movie, "Nothing but the Truth," was playing at the Carolina the night of this 1941 photograph. —*Courtesy, Tommy Acker*

Mondays and Thursdays when he would rush to a center aisle seat on row eight or nine to catch the one o'clock matinee of every new film.

In early 1941, some months after the Palmetto's opening, the Carolina closed for a week for a complete refurbishing. New blue-green carpet was laid and new, more comfortable seats (identical to those in the Palmetto) were installed. A few decorations were replaced but no structural changes resulted, and patrons came back to a fresh theatre with a different color scheme that retained its former appeal. The renovation did not, however, extend to the segregated balcony, where the original Montgomery seats would remain indefinitely, and no resilient new carpet would greet the patrons of the upper reaches of the theatre.

~*6*~

The World War II Years and the Aftermath

t the beginning of World War II, theatres remained an essential part of a city's image and pride. When the South Carolina Writers' Project published *South Carolina: A Guide to the Palmetto State* in 1941 (under W.P.A. sponsorship), profiles of the larger cities in the state included the number of hotels, radio stations, and motion picture theatres as basic amenities and indicators of social and economic standing. The Carolina and the new Palmetto continued to enhance the theatrical experience as uniformed doormen and ushers greeted the patrons, and the feature film always began with the dimming of footlights and a parting curtain. At the State and Strand, the staffs were smaller and dressed in suits or sport jackets, but the comfort of the ticket buyer was still foremost. It was still a time when people were more likely to say, "I'm going to the Carolina (or State)" rather than "I'm going to see a Clark Gable film."

Spartanburg had its final taste of genuine theatrical grandeur when Tallulah Bankhead brought *The Little Foxes* to the Carolina's stage on February 24, 1941. Over the years, many Broadway successes had come to town in well-cast, stylish productions, but seldom had Spartans had an

CAROLINA

THEATRE

SPARTANBURG
ONE PERFORMANCE ONLY

TOMORROW!

FEB. 24th

One of the greatest plays of the
generation with a cast that sets
a new standard of excellence.

HERMAN SHUMLIN
has the honor to present

TALLULAH BANKHEAD
in

THE LITTLE FOXES

LILLIAN HELLMAN'S Dramatic Triumph
with FRANK CONROY
and a distinguished Broadway cast

A Few Choice
Seats Available
In Orchestra
At $2.40
and $3.00

All Prices Include Taxes

HURRY! GET YOUR
TICKETS EARLY!

opportunity to see a play of the calibre of Lillian Hellman's uncompromising *The Little Foxes.* Just as Katharine Cornell had made the role of Elizabeth Barrett Browning her own, Bankhead would make Regina Giddens her signature role. On December 17 of the same year (ten days after Pearl Harbor and the entry of the United States into World War II) another production, *Life with Father*, with a cast headed by the well-known actors Dorothy Gish and Louis Calherne, played the Carolina—and in this case, there would be both matinee and evening performances. *Life with Father* had opened on Broadway in 1939, and by the time it finally closed, it would have had a total of over 3,200 performances. This would be the last major touring production seen in Spartanburg until near the end of World War II. Throughout the war years, the only other live appearances would be an occasional swing band that performed with a vocalist on a simply dressed stage. The accompanying film fare was inevitably a mediocre "B" picture that filled in the gaps between the several live performances during the matinee and evening. When required, the white grand piano that resided in a prop room at stage right would be tuned and wheeled onstage and off between the live performances and the film screenings.

An Army camp had changed the social and economic life of Spartanburg a generation earlier; now the presence of Camp Croft and its trainees transformed the life of the city once again. Finally, Sunday movies were permitted—at least after church hours—with a matinee at 2 p.m. and an evening showing at 8 p.m. More often than not the Carolina was filled to capacity, with lines for the next show sometimes stretching from the lobby entrance, down the hallway in the Montgomery Building, and out on the street at the northern entrance. The theatres on Main Street prospered, too, and the Palmetto began to hold over in the Sunday-Monday-Tuesday slot the film that had played the Carolina the previous week. The war also had an immediate effect on the operations of the theatres as well. Most of the ushers, doormen, and assistant managers were drafted into the Army. Younger ushers were eager to be hired, but women now had opportunities to rise from box-office cashier to assistant manager jobs. Young women in ordinary attire replaced the uniformed doormen at the Carolina, and at the Strand, Catharine Hamby became the city's first woman theatre manager. The look of downtown streets changed slightly, too, when someone had the misguided idea of donating the city's graceful cast-iron street lamps to the war effort and replaced them with concrete replicas crowned by twin neon tubes. No one found the results appealing, and a few law-abiding citizens contemplated vandalism.

In 1943, the Camp Croft all-soldier show *Ten Minute Break*, conceived by Private David Reid and Corporal Millard Thomson, was booked for an evening performance at the Carolina, but at the last minute it was shifted (and sandwiched onto) the stage at the State because some moral arbiters decided that it was too risqué for

Spartanburg's premier showplace. Just who actually decreed the switch is unclear, but it did deprive many potential ticket buyers of a chance to see a rousing satirical musical revue at a time when live entertainment was a rarity. The State was filled to capacity, with standees wherever a space existed, and the large cast of professional and non-professional actors from the ranks of trainees at Camp Croft overflowed the tiny dressing rooms into the area behind the theatre on Broad Street.

There was, to be sure, some pointed humor and double-entendre at the expense of local customs and suggestions that life in Spartanburg was not nearly as conventional as many might have preferred. And then there was drag—not just a vaudeville-type specialty act but also a chorus line of young GIs who may have seemed all too genuine. Perhaps no one in the audience suspected that a lead performer named Zero Mostel would become the most acclaimed comic actor of the American stage in the postwar years. David Reid, another drafted professional actor, would return to town after the war and establish the city's most enduring community theatre—based, perhaps ironically, at one of Camp Croft's old movie houses. *Ten Minute Break* was not the first all-soldier show to be seen in Spartanburg;

The State was announcing a film, "We Go Fast" and stage performances of a touring variety show, "Powder and Lipstick," when this photograph was taken in 1941.
—*Courtesy, Tommy Acker*

Camp Wadsworth's *You Know Me Al!* and Fort Jackson's *As You Were* had played the Harris in 1918, but America had seen a revolution in dress, behavior, entertainment media, and modes of travel in the interim. Why the earlier Camp Wadsworth show, with its bevy of soldiers in drag and innuendo had played on the stage of the leading playhouse with wide acceptance and this production, its clear descendant, was denied access to the Carolina stage will probably remain only partially told. No one has yet rescued the scripts of these all-male military shows (if they still exist) to make comparisons.

Casablanca, The Maltese Falcon, and *Now, Voyager* were all booked into three-day, early-week, less desirable slots at the Carolina, for at the time of their original release no one could have imagined their durability and continued popularity some sixty years later. They all drew respectable audiences, but it was the patriotic blockbusters *Sergeant York* and *Mrs. Miniver* that filled the house to capacity and had lines of ticket-holders waiting during their weeklong runs. The theatre operators were smiling as they removed the previous night's box-office take from the safe in the assistant manager's office and deposited it in the bank in the Andrews Building each morning. Businesses adjacent to the theatres prospered too. The small drugstore beside the Carolina's entrance dispensed soft drinks from its stylish soda fountain and watched theatregoers snatch up candy bars and egg-salad sandwiches from the counter. The Blue Bird Ice Cream parlor just south on North Church was also a popular stopover before or after a film; knowing teenagers preferred Turner's Store, across the street, where roasted peanuts—as well as secondhand movie magazines—cost only a nickel. On Main Street the small popcorn shop in the building that housed the Strand kept busy from mid-morning until 9 p.m. replenishing its supply of freshly popped, buttered corn. Its likes would never be tasted in future years when theatres would sell their own pre-popped variety. Nor would later audiences know the subtle aroma emitted by the highly flammable

The flashing marquee of the Carolina gleamed on North Church Street from 1932, when Wilby-Kincey installed it, until the 1970s. This photo was taken in 1939.
—*Courtesy, Spartanburg County Historical Association*

nitrate film that seemed to permeate the smaller movie theatres. In the late 1940s non-flammable film stock would be introduced, and eventually bulbs would replace the carbon arcs in the projectors that gave the real meaning to "the silver screen."

Spartans had a chance to see a few movie actors in the flesh during the war years. Betty Grable came to Camp Croft to entertain the troops, and Jane Wyman (not yet a major star) and the new heartthrob John Payne arrived to sell war bonds. When they appeared before the microphones set up at the western end of the bandstand in Morgan Square, the huge crowd was enthusiastic. They spent the night at the Cleveland Hotel, where local dignitaries had a chance to rub shoulders with Hollywood celebrities. A year later, Jeanette MacDonald registered at the Cleveland, too, before her recital at Twichell Auditorium the following night. She decided to see a movie at the Carolina, arrived unannounced, and was almost unnoticed in spite of her famous red hair.

The early 1940s were also a time of food, clothing, and gasoline rationing; there was constant concern for sons, husbands, and daughters who were in various branches of the military service, and apprehension about the slow (though steady) progress of the Allies against the Nazis in Europe and Africa and the Japanese in the Pacific. Just as the last remnants of Hitler's army were surrendering, Americans were stunned to hear the radio reports of the death of President Franklin Roosevelt, just a few months into his historic fourth term. He had been the first president to reach out to the country by radio, and his figure was familiar throughout the war in the newsreels at the four theatres. Now Spartans watched somberly the newsreel shots of the train bearing the president's body from Georgia to Washington—a train that had passed through Spartanburg, where townspeople, some of them weeping openly, had lined the Southern tracks. A few months later, the first atomic bomb would be dropped, and then the second. Peace was at hand.

In May 1945, the Carolina was able to book its first fully-staged production in more than three years, and it was quite appropriately a nostalgic look at an operetta by a composer who had been a local favorite years before. Victor Herbert's *Naughty Marietta* was familiar to many moviegoers through the popular MGM film of 1935, which had returned to town twice after its initial run at the Carolina. A few in attendance may even have seen it on the Harris stage in 1912, when Oscar Hammerstein's production came to town boasting sixty vocalists. The show was a sellout and for many younger ticket holders it was their first experience of live musical theatre. And many were seeing for the first time the now-faded front fire curtain with its Montgomery logo still stenciled on in blue. Although no one suspected at the time, it would be the last professional production of an operetta in Spartanburg—at least in the twentieth century.

In 1948, Diana Barrymore (daughter of John and niece of Lionel and Ethel) appeared in a touring production of *Joan of Lorraine* by respected playwright Maxwell Anderson. It was quite unlike the conventional three-act plays that most Spartans knew. There were entrances from the house (on a runway placed over the orchestra pit at one side), and a number of the actors played multiple roles. Furthermore, it was presented as a rehearsal of a play about Joan of Arc and contained pointed political commentary about the contemporary world. With Ingrid Bergman in the lead in New York, it had been a Broadway success, but the roadshow version with Barrymore was far short of a sellout in Spartanburg. The following year, a more visible star, Sylvia Sidney, was somewhat more successful in *O Mistress Mine*, a more conventional, sophisticated comedy by Terrence Rattigan. It was not a sellout either, but it was much more to the taste of Spartanburg audiences. Its lead was also a seasoned stage performer (and movie star) who was able to project her persona to the balcony.

For these postwar performances the theatrical ambiance was somewhat diminished. The Montgomery theatre fire curtain that greeted the audience was now faded and dusty; the velvet front curtain had been replaced by a beige sateen curtain that was designed more to cover a movie screen than to part or rise to reveal a stage set. The handout programs had never been elaborate, but they had once featured ads for local businesses and provided information on the theatre's facilities. Now they were a simple sheet with names of cast and actors and the acts and scenes, with intermission(s) indicated. Above all, the air of expectation that had often pervaded the theatre was either missing or diminished. Local newspaper coverage, when it existed at all, was polite reporting on the event. It was indeed a far cry from the era of the Opera House, when Spartans could read brief but perceptive critiques of the week's theatre fare in at least one of the local newspapers.

The return of Tallulah Bankhead in a revival of Noel Coward's *Private Lives* on December 6, 1950, would prove to be the last fully-staged production to play the Carolina stage in the twentieth century. By this time, the South's most acclaimed actress had become a caricature of herself in the eyes of many. But it was this exaggerated image that probably sold more tickets than the play itself. A much-anticipated performance of the Broadway musical *Brigadoon* was booked the following year, but a rail strike prevented the company from ever reaching Spartanburg. Many disappointed ticket-holders got refunds, and the theatre management was hardly encouraged to try again. At least 1950 was a good year for movies: two "has-beens" in the eyes of movie exhibitors returned in triumph—Bette Davis in *All about Eve*, and Gloria Swanson in *Sunset Boulevard*. However, few imagined when these films played a few days each at the Carolina that fifty years later they would be the ones that would be re-released in pristine prints to delight audiences in another century and become perennials on cable TV.

~7~

The Rest of the Story

adio had offered strong competition to the movies in the 1930s, but it was nothing to compare with the inroads that television would make in luring audiences away from theatres after 1950. Instead of a night out at the movies, millions now stayed home to watch sitcoms, variety shows, and game shows on their small black-and-white living room screens. Late night films became a regular feature on local channels, and Spartans watched, in spite of the annoying commercials. The theatres would still have a monopoly on color for more than a decade, but they also tried new weapons in the battle. The Palmetto exploited 3-D films during their short period of popularity and handed out a pair of cardboard glasses at the door to every patron. In 1953, the Carolina installed the city's first cinemascope screen to show the biblical epic *The Robe* and the many releases that followed in the new ratio. Since its proscenium was thirty-six feet wide, the slightly curved screen fit easily into the space; but single speaker horns were no longer sufficient, and the triple speakers behind the screen now made fully-staged plays impractical or even impossible. The State soon followed suit with a new wide screen placed comfortably within the proscenium frame.

For the Palmetto, the wide-screen format was never satisfactory. The auditorium tapered down to a proscenium that was a perfect frame for the standard 1:1.33 picture ratio, and the only way to show films in wide screen was to lower the screen masking to create a lower and wider frame, and in the process creating a smaller screen. It did not go unnoticed by audiences, and it marked the beginning of the Palmetto's decline.

The new Spartanburg Memorial Auditorium opened on North Church Street in 1951. It was appropriately designated an "auditorium" rather than a "theatre," since

A young Spartan and his date head for the Palmetto box office on a rainy afternoon in the 1950s. —*Courtesy, author's collection*

its very size made it unsuited for traditional stage presentations. Like most of the multipurpose facilities built at the time, the new entertainment center had serious drawbacks for many kinds of live performances—though it was decidedly more functional than the barnlike Textile Hall in Greenville (which would soon be replaced by a more comfortable facility). In the first few seasons the attractions were quite ambitious and varied, ranging from ballet to solo recitals. Hoping to increase its membership, the Civic Music Association moved its series from Twichell Auditorium (famed for its remarkable acoustics) to the much larger and less suitable facility. When the booming voice of Leonard Warren, which could reach the uppermost tier of the original Metropolitan Opera House, seemed remote and unimpressive from many areas of the auditorium, it was apparent that only amplified performances were likely to succeed in the space. Civic Music soon returned to its original home.

While the comfortable new auditorium provided a stage for touring attractions, it was not a theatre in the sense that the Opera House or the Harris had been in their day, offering a weekly program of performances where no alternative (or competition) existed. Nor did it provide steady employment for stagehands, billposters, and musicians, while bringing business to downtown hotels and restaurants from early fall to late spring. Bookings were intermittent, and the habit of theatre-going on a regular basis was a thing of the past. Occasionally a major touring production could be booked with local sponsorship. The Goodfellows were responsible for the one-night stand of an adaptation of Stephen Vincent Benet's *John Brown's Body* on January 6, 1954. Movie stars Tyrone Power, Anne Baxter, and Raymond Massey "read" the narrative passages, accompanied by an eighteen-member chorus, soloists, and dancers. It was an unusual dramatic concept directed by Charles Laughton, and it attracted a large audience. Still, its impact would have been far greater in a theatre of the Carolina's dimensions.

In the 1960s, a new phenomenon in touring brought musicals to smaller cities like Spartanburg. Rehearsed in New York, pared-down versions of Broadway hits now took to the road in the so-called "truck and bus" companies. With the aid of amplification, which had enabled many smaller-voiced performers to succeed in traditional theatres, these companies brought reasonable facsimiles of the real thing to larger municipal facilities like Spartanburg's auditorium—although their bookings would be widely spaced.

In 1953, Max Greenewald died at the age of eighty-three, having survived his older brother Isaac by some six years. His obituary made the front page of *The Herald* but contained not a line about his involvement in Spartanburg's theatrical life as a young man. Memory was becoming short—or at least careless. Max had witnessed the evolution of popular entertainment from gas-lit live melodrama to television; when he contemplated the changes that technology had wrought, he surely felt a tinge of nostalgia for the exciting times when a new show came to town almost every night. Both brothers had possessed remarkable artistic talent, business acumen, and a sense of civic responsibility. They had been active members of the local chapters of national or international fraternal orders. Max was a member of the Improved Order of Red Man, and Isaac had become Exalted Ruler of the Benevolent and Protective Order of Elks. No participants in Spartanburg's growth from village to city made more important contributions to its cultural, financial, and retail vitality; but their remains were returned to Wilmington, the first stop of their parents in their migration south from Philadelphia.

Audiences had never been monolithic, and movie exhibitors in Spartanburg had in essence acknowledged that fact by scheduling action and western films on weekends, while the dramas known as "women's pictures" were often relegated to a two-day, early-week stand. The diversity grew in the 1950s, as imported films from Europe and Japan began to attract cultural notice. But these films had the stigma of subtitles, and the decidedly off-putting label of "art film" only contributed to their scarcity of bookings outside the larger cities. One Wilby-Kincey movie theatre in Charlotte (the Dilworth) did in fact begin to book foreign releases—although the English comedies of Alec Guinness were more in evidence than the masterpieces of Kurosawa. Eager to see a greater spectrum of film entertainment, a group of local people, spurred by Norwood and Monique Harrison, created the Spartanburg Fine Film Committee and worked closely with Kerr McBride, the new manager of the struggling Palmetto, to book films that would bypass the city without some sort of endorsement or special promotion.

The first series opened on February 24, 1954, with a two-day run of the American film *The Member of the Wedding* (which would not have been shown in Spartanburg without the Committee's seal of approval). Two months later, a genuine foreign film with subtitles was shown; it was the now-classic *Forbidden Games*. One of the most successful of all would be a re-release of Garbo's most acclaimed film, *Camille*, the following year. Not all of the more than forty selections of the first three seasons were actually first-rate, and British comedies and mysteries far outnumbered the French, Italian, Russian, and Japanese titles; but they provided a welcome alternative to bookings at the Carolina and State (both now first-run houses operated by different companies). Unfortunately, the Palmetto was now dingy, and linoleum had replaced the worn red carpet in the aisles; and there were problems involving the different film ratios. The projectors at the theatre had acquired new wide-screen apertures, and changing back to the old 1:1.33 ratio in which many of the imported pictures and revivals were shot was a nuisance to the projectionists. The first matinee of the Bolshoi Ballet's *Romeo and Juliet* featured dancing in which the feet were invisible with a wide screen aperture. Only an urgent appeal from the chairman of the Fine Film Committee got the correct aperture in place. No one had considered that bringing subtitled films in a foreign language to the Palmetto's screen would have anything but a positive effect, but the culture shock was too great for some young, casual ticket buyers who were so perplexed by what they saw (and heard) on screen that they left the theatre indignantly. Reading at the movies was not for them.

A few years before demolition of the Palmetto Theatre in 2003, the marquee advertised the arts community of Spartanburg. An office building was later constructed here. —*Courtesy, Mark Olencki*

Although live performances now seemed a thing of the past for the Carolina, the theatre was indeed able to find room onstage in 1956 for a larger-than-life rising musical star who would soon become a cultural icon and change the course of American popular music. He was, of course, Elvis Presley. If the stage hangings were now ratty and faded, it mattered little to the enthusiastic young audience that crowded into the theatre to see their hero. Decades later, many mature Spartans would recall the event nostalgically and with a sense of having been witnesses to entertainment history. It might have occurred to the theatre management that bookings of other entertainers less dynamic than Presley might still provide an economic boost to the declining income from motion picture exhibition, but nothing was invested in upgrading the

Carolina's stage mechanisms and lighting, which had hardly changed in thirty years. Still, for all the wear and tear since the 1941 refurbishing, the theatre itself retained a unique elegance and grandeur.

A decade after the famous Presley visit, the Carolina would lose its longtime manager Robert (Bob) Talbert, who had shared the same birthplace, Tupelo, Mississippi, as Presley. No manager in the Wilby-Kincey empire had enjoyed longer tenure at one of the company's major theatres. When Talbert succumbed to cancer in 1966 at the age of fifty-seven, he had been overseeing the business and operations of the house for thirty-three years. Like the Greenewalds, his managerial predecessors from an earlier age, he had joined a civic organization to make a personal contribution to the city's progress; at his funeral, members of the local Lions Club were honorary pallbearers. For several generations of ushers and other employees he had been "Mr. T," and none could forget his natty attire, his slow but deliberate movement across the Carolina's lobby—or his capacity for devastating rebuke if someone carelessly detracted from the classy ambience of his ship of state. Because of his guarded demeanor around employees it was difficult to know whether Bob Talbert was much of a movie or stage fan himself, but his refined sensibility to the magical effect of theatre ambience prevented any structural damage to a theatre he loved during his lifetime. To many he may have seemed wedded to his profession, but in later years, his son, journalist Robert B. Talbert, Jr., would write affectingly about the personal side of a man who sometimes escaped on fishing trips with one of the Carolina's projectionists, Henry Childress. Unfortunately, a few years after his death, the theatre would close its doors.

In the final years of the 1960s, Spartanburg's Main Street was losing its business to shopping centers and malls. The city's prime department store, Aug. W. Smith's, would depart, along with Belk-Hudson and Greenewald's; only Prices' and Woolworth's reminded the remaining shoppers of the thriving commercial center that had been.

The Palmetto was reduced to showing Kung Fu movies and even soft-core pornography in its dismal interior; the State would undergo a tasteful and non-destructive revamping in 1970, only to be partly destroyed in an early morning fire not long afterwards. Its life with its new name, the Capri, would be brief. The Carolina underwent a similar though unnecessarily destructive revamping, but its new marquee was the only lit sign to be seen in the vicinity of the Montgomery Building. The windows of all the shops that faced North Church Street had been walled up, and none was now a commercial store or pharmacy. The honored custom of window-shopping before and after a movie was now long abandoned, as was the healthy practice of walking to a movie. The cinder-block mall cinemas (and the multiplexes that, in turn, succeeded them) could only be reached by car, and they had no individual names (as befitted their generic interiors). Never again would anyone casually say: "I'm going to the Strand." Or, yes, "to the Magic" of lost memory.

In the 1960s and 1970s, moviegoing moved to nondescript theatres in the suburbs. The Pinewood Cinema was among the first of these.
—Courtesy, B&B Studio

~ Epilogue ~

Archeology, Requiems, and Restorations

he destinies of theatres in the United States
have more often than not been determined by
economic cycles, changes in taste, and land
values. The magical palaces, large and small, that
flourished until technology depleted their audiences were
almost always built by business entrepreneurs who
received a percentage of their ticket sales. Still, in the eyes
of the audiences, the Opera Houses, Academies of Music,
as well as theatres like the Harris, took on a distinctive
civic identity. Although Spartanburg's Opera House was
actually part of a municipal building (and a very eye-
pleasing one at that), it was leased as a business venture to
private operators. When its seating capacity became
inadequate for profitability, the city fathers themselves
decreed its destruction—with no malicious intent but little
foresight. The Harris, the Lester, the Rex, and the
Montgomery, along with the smaller movie-vaudeville
theatres, were all privately built by investors or individuals
such as J. T. Harris, C. L. Henry, and the Montgomery
family, but they belonged to everyone who bought a ticket.

In most ways, the theatrical life of Spartanburg
replicated that of dozens of other small cities in the
Southeast. The touring companies that followed the rail

lines were, after all, the same, and Greenville or Asheville was usually the next stop. Shows that played at the Opera House or the Harris had often had bookings in Charlotte, Salisbury, or Greensboro a few nights before. Other cities had their manager-impresario equivalents of Max and Isaac Greenewald. Whether they could approach their unique combination of artistic talent and business acumen is another matter. Certainly, the "Greenewald touch" made a difference in some choices of bookings and in their manner of promotion and presentation. In all the neighboring cities, someone was ready to step up and invest in that new entertainment craze, the movies, and they built small and large theatres to show them (hopefully, for a profit). In Spartanburg, it was Lawrence Lester, Jr., whose second "house beautiful" was the incomparable and enduring Strand—a theatre with no exact equivalent in those other cities.

In addition to the lively entertainments in the theatres, Spartanburg had a decided cultural plus in the yearly spring Southeastern Music Festival, which brought some of the world's greatest musical talent to Converse College's Twichell Auditorium. Where else at that time (or since) in the Carolinas could a performance of the Verdi Requiem have front-page headlines as large as those for the sinking of the Lusitania? If hardship abounded for many citizens and sickness could come swiftly and often fatally in an age when penicillin and vaccines for childhood diseases did not exist, a rich cultural life thrived in the small city where the statue of Daniel Morgan still looked nobly toward Cowpens.

It is perhaps remarkable that the Strand (Lester) flourished on East Main Street under different ownerships for thirty-three years with no significant assault on its architecture and ambience. The Rex, with only a hiatus of four years during the Depression, would do even better, enduring more than fifty years. The Palmetto, the newest and, sadly, least adaptable, would stand for more than sixty years (gradually deteriorating for half that time) but never be given a redecoration that might have made it more inviting. In the first decade of the new century, only the Montgomery/Carolina remains intact and restorable in spite of the senseless damage it suffered in the harmful remodeling. The closing of the theatres would be reflected in the disappearance of the full page devoted to entertainment every Sunday in the *Herald-Journal*—a page that many readers had turned to first to see what films (or stage entertainments) would be available in the coming week, or read a promotional article on a new film or stage celebrity.

Even as the curtain was coming down on an era of live entertainment and theatres were disappearing, interest was growing in restoring downtown showplaces as venues for live performance and, in some instances, music centers. Fortunately, there are quite a few surviving and beautifully restored theatres within a 200-mile radius of Spartanburg. In Augusta, the Imperial (the same vintage as the Rex but larger) has been exquisitely restored and is a popular venue for a variety of touring entertainments as well as the Augusta Opera. Three "Carolinas" in North Carolina cities have received new leases on life. Winston-Salem's Carolina, in a rather drastic reconfiguration that preserved its interior décor, has become the Stevens Center for the Performing Arts; Greensboro's imposing Carolina has received a very faithful restoration, complete with the preserved Wurlitzer, and is a successful venue for live entertainment and film retrospectives. Similarly, the Carolina in Durham has been attractively returned to its original appearance. Thanks to the Spoleto Festival, Charleston's vaudeville house, the Garden, has been refurbished and its stage modernized for contemporary productions. Older Opera Houses survive and function in tiny Abbeville and in Macon (which had a thriving theatre life long before Spartanburg). South Carolina's most remarkable success story in restoration is Newberry's Opera House, which resembles Spartanburg's long lost theatre on the square and dates from the same period. Not only has the restored auditorium given the city a venue for a variety of entertainments and local uses, it has transformed the cultural life of the city in ways that no one could have anticipated. Thirty-five years ago, the Newberry Opera House was an empty, seatless hall with only traces of its original décor. Amazingly, the original painted canvas drop curtain with ads for local businesses hung askew behind the proscenium, and beyond that a sole surviving but faded canvas drop with a pastoral scene hung from the flies. Today that ghostly ambience has been transformed into an interior of striking beauty whose lights gleam throughout the year.

By no means the least significant restoration (or perhaps transformation) has taken place right in Spartanburg. It is Converse College's Twichell Auditorium, which was not included in the story of the city's theatres because it was not constructed as a theatre but as a concert hall without lighting and provisions for scenery, and also because it was not a part of the commercial area. It is true that college and semi-professional opera performances were staged there over the years, but it only became a theatre in the strictest sense through a total reconstruction of its interior in the 1990s. The original look of Twichell was austere, and intrusive metal pillars supported its three-sided balcony. What it lacked in theatrical grandeur seemed unimportant to those hearing musical performances with unequaled clarity. While the new auditorium is in the "spirit" of the original, its look is more striking, and it now has a modern stage housing and lighting. That it retains much of the famed acoustical superiority of the old Twichell is miraculous, and, equally miraculous, is the genuine theatre "magic" that it now radiates.

Theatre has proven to be resilient in the United States in spite of the competition for audiences with films, television, and the Internet. In the final decades of the twentieth century, not-for-profit regional theatre companies were established in virtually every major

American city from Atlanta to San Diego. As the movement spread to smaller cities, some companies would perform in the very heart of downtowns that had been drained of commerce by shopping malls and multiplex cinemas. Some performed in theatres that had once been objects of civic pride, with names like Majestic, State, Imperial, and Paramount; others transformed abandoned buildings into smaller performance spaces, where their contracts with professional unions are determined by actual seating capacity. The more successful in fundraising, like Atlanta's Alliance Theatre, were able to build new state-of-the-art facilities that would become the focus of civic pride much as the Opera Houses and Academies of Music had been a century before. Depending on a core of subscription supporters, these often adventurous companies are seldom free of financial constraints as they plan a season of four or five plays that will have runs of three to six weeks. The era of the one-night stands and actors enduring grueling travel as they moved from one city to the next is over; and, sadly, so is the rich variety of shows once available across America from September to May. But the new resident companies are successfully introducing new audiences to the unique experience of an audience interacting with live performers.

Charlotte now has more than one functioning professional theatre company, and Greenville is home to the nationally recognized Warehouse Theatre with a reputation for offering a varied season and sometimes risky productions of plays without a Broadway cachet. It seems inevitable that a cadre of enterprising young theatre professionals will at some point take up residence in the reviving center of Spartanburg to add to the mix of live entertainment provided by the community theatre and infrequent touring performers. If Spartanburg's Montgomery/Carolina Theatre is recovered as a venue for live performance and film festivals, then once again will there be a thriving nightlife in the heart of the city, complemented by the commercial establishments it attracts. One smaller South Carolina city, Newberry, has already experienced a cultural and economic revival thanks to the restoration of its Opera House (a contemporary of Spartanburg's original showplace). It was and is once more: the Opera House.

By luck, or civic imagination, Spartanburg acquired an architecturally distinguished theatre that would rival all the performance spaces of its size in the Southeast and remain the city's pride for decades. Now its stage is dark and not even the traditional, single "ghost light" dispels the shadows, but its proscenium is intact and even the old Montgomery fire curtain, with its stenciled design, is still in place. With another stroke of luck, and civic imagination, it will gleam again and become a new cultural magnet.

Theatre Spaces:
From the Opera House
to the Palmetto

heatres were built in downtown Spartanburg—and sometimes quickly converted to other uses—from the 1880s until
1940, when the last motion picture theatre, the Palmetto,
opened at the corner of East Main and North Liberty streets.
While interior photographs of many remain undiscovered, Sanborn
Insurance Maps of the city confirm their location and size. Seating
capacities and stage dimensions and facilities for the Opera House and the
Harris, constructed exclusively for live performances, are documented in
the Julius Cahn national theatre guides, and details on moving picture
houses were added in the later Julius Cahn-Gus Hill directories. A seating
plan of the Montgomery/Carolina confirms the specific number of seats in
that theatre. Seating capacities for several of the other theatres are listed
in motion picture trade directories, but the figures are frequently
inaccurate and are not included in these profiles of the theatres, which
document their basic design, operations, and locations, and destinies.

The Opera House ~

Spartanburg's first real theatre, constructed in the 1880s, occupied
the entire second floor of a municipal building that also housed the city's
post office on the first floor. Erected to produce revenue, as well as to
provide a stage for touring theatre companies and civic events, private
operators leased it periodically through sealed bids. The oldest surviving
photograph shows the building, with its stately clock tower, overlooking
an assortment of farmers' wagons, probably on a Saturday morning. By
1907, the year in which the Opera House closed, the entire area was
paved with brick, and streetcars ran beside the Daniel Morgan statue to
turn right into Magnolia Street.

The local Opera House resembled the surviving (and now beautifully restored) Opera House in Newberry, with its large proscenium and painted canvas drop curtain. The seating capacity was roughly the same: 700 for the Spartanburg theatre and 732 for Newberry. In addition, there was a standee area, which increased the capacity of the house to about 800 for the frequently sold-out performances. The parquet, or orchestra, section featured a dress circle of perhaps two or three rows that commanded top ticket prices; on the second level there was a balcony dress circle (slightly cheaper) and behind (or above) that a gallery, where seats often went for as little as 25 cents.

The stage opening of the theatre was 28 x 30 feet, with a stage depth of 30 feet and total backstage width of 60 feet—a fairly spacious performance space. A stairway at the rear of the building led to the stage door, and some space at street level provided storage space for the theatre's own supply of scenery and props: perspectives painted on canvas for outdoor scenes and flats that fitted into grooves on the stage to create varied side frames as well as interior rooms. Spartanburg's Opera House had been converted from gas lighting to electricity, and arc lights and limelight were used to enhance or spot performers. The interior of the auditorium was decorated in blue and red, and after the availability of electricity it featured rows of gleaming bulbs to light the auditorium. Outside, a large display board at the base of the clock tower featured posters of current and coming shows. At the beginning of the century, tickets went on sale early at Greenewald's, further up on the square, and one-sheets and larger printed displays were posted around town. The theatre closed permanently at the end of the 1906-07 season and was torn down a few months later.

The Magic and the Fairyland ~

Lawrence Lester, Jr. opened the Magic and Fairyland nickelodeons on Magnolia Street in 1905. Both of these early movie theatres were situated in existing buildings on the east side of Magnolia, just north of Morgan Square, and both remained in business until the opening of the larger Lyric Theatre on East Main in 1909. The Magic was located at 115 Magnolia, in the first building behind the large retail store facing the square, and a lateral electric sign on a pole proclaimed "Magic" in large letters. It did not extend the entire depth of the structure, and a printing business operated in the rear. Eventually, the building became one of the most interesting secondhand stores in Spartanburg, where old books, furniture, postcards, and other memorabilia were on sale. Although all traces of the theatre's interior vanished after its closing, the word "Magic" remained set in octagonal tiles, black on white, in the raked entranceway, and even after the razing of the building in the 1970s, the name of the theatre was visible for a while as a ghostly reminder of a past era.

The Fairyland was located only a few doors from the Magic, at 121 Magnolia, in a structure that was somewhat deeper than the Magic's, but possibly narrower. Both theatres advertised continuous showings of programs of one-reelers from 2 p.m. until 9 p.m. in the evening. At the Fairyland, refreshments were also sold.

The Harris Theatre ~

The construction of the Harris Theatre in 1907 was at least second-page news for several months, with its progress reported in both *The Herald* and *The Journal*. If it were not for these detailed accounts, it would be difficult to recreate mentally the interior and facilities of the large and impressive showplace that once stood on the southeast corner of North Church and Elm (St. John) streets. As early as May 24, 1907, some details of the new building were reported: the front section would be three stories, with twenty office rooms on the second and third floors, and the main floor would have a lunchroom, a music house, and a ticket office. The middle and rear walls (later to prove the theatre's undoing) were to be carried thirty or forty feet higher under the supervision of the construction's contractor, W. L. Cannon. With its spacious orchestra and two balconies that circled the auditorium, it would be one of the largest and best-equipped theatres in the Carolinas. An added bonus for the lessees of the third-floor offices on the north side was an unobstructed view of the mountains in the distance.

The stage was one of the largest in the South at that time, with a total width of 80 feet, a depth of 40 feet from the footlights; the distance from stage to gridiron was 55 feet and the depth under the stage was 10 feet; the proscenium itself was 38 x 35 feet and framed by stage boxes. A hundred pieces of scenery were commissioned from the Garring Scenic Company (headquarters in Buffalo and Atlanta), which was also painting scenery for the even larger Academy of Music in Charlotte. By September 12, the fireproof front curtain had been delivered and installed. It was painted to imitate rich plush, and the spaces for advertisements (obviously still a practice in 1907) were light cream color, with heavy gold filigrees; the lettering was in navy blue, with letters shaded in gold. This spectacular drop curtain weighed in at 1,000 pounds, and 300 pounds of fireproof paint had been required to complete it. The three-story front exterior of the building was of yellow brick, with stone trimmings and a prefabricated metal overhang at the top. The twin entrance arches in the center did not actually suggest the grand theatre that lay beyond, and, oddly, the theatre did not have a lateral or horizontal electric sign with its name. Only a pole with a few electric lanterns hung over the entrance, and a one-sheet poster easel outside advertised the current offering.

Julius Cahn's Theatre Directory gives the seating capacity of the Harris as 1,200, though the words "ground floor" follow that figure. Since the newspaper accounts give 1,800 as the capacity, it is possible that Cahn's figure did not include the seats in the two large balconies. Very often seating estimates included standing room, and no doubt the Harris could accommodate at least 100 standees, if not more. In addition to employing a larger staff than the old Opera House, the Harris spent more on advertising space on billboards and poster stands, ranging from one-sheets to 24 sheets on occasion (posted by the Southern Advertising Company). The W.F. Barnes printing company had a standing order for programs—often for as many as six different shows in a week.

For some twelve years, including the period of World War I, the Harris was the showplace of Spartanburg; but in 1920, the auditorium was condemned, reportedly because of deteriorating brick in its walls. The huge stage and part of the interior were razed, and a new rear wall constructed for the remaining section of the building. The retail and office parts of the building would remain for decades and would only completely disappear with the widening of St. John (Elm) Street and the construction of a drive-in bank where part of the theatre had stood.

The Electric, the Globe, the Royal Palace, the Dixie (and others) ~

Between 1907 and 1918, at least eight small theatres opened on Kennedy Place, South Liberty, Magnolia, and along the block on North Church between Kennedy Place and Commerce Street, but with one possible exception all were in existing buildings that were adapted for motion picture exhibition. Most were short-lived and the buildings reverted to retail or other use. Around 1908, the Southern Amusement Company opened the Electric at 110 Kennedy Place. It was a small nickelodeon space that the operators no doubt hoped would give competition to Lawrence Lester's successful Magic and Fairyland, but within a year or so the theatre closed and the space became a music store. In 1909, a certain Edney Ridge, living at the Argyle Hotel, sponsored a contest to name the new theatre that he was opening at 145 North Church. It was a narrow theatre with a small stage and officially opened as the Royal Palace. It offered matinees and evenings of vaudeville acts at an admission price of only ten cents and was managed by W. E. Baker. This was first of several theatres that offered cut-rate live entertainment; with no more than 300 seats (or less), it seemed an unlikely candidate for financial success. In no time, the Royal Palace had closed, and a substitute, the Royal, had opened across the street at 156 North Church. Lawrence Lester also opened Spartanburg's first black theatre, the Globe, at 190 South Liberty, near the Southern Railroad crossing. In 1913, yet another small vaudeville house, the Vandette, operated for a short time at 137 Magnolia Street. During the period of World War I, when several thousand black recruits were in training at Camp Wadsworth, two new "colored" theatres opened at 136 and 139 North Church, at the corner of Commerce Street. The larger of the two was the Dixie, and it is possible that the building was designed and built as a theatre. It survived into the 1920s. It was eventually replaced by a rather seedy five-and-ten-cent store. The Dunbar at the other location moved to a new auditorium on Short Wofford Street in the 1920s and was later renamed the Union. Yet another short-lived theatre, the Bonita, opened at 169 West Main (opposite the Cleveland Hotel) during the prosperous years of 1917-18. All of these "forgotten" theatres required a substantial investment for seats, decoration, projection equipment and a fireproof projection booth, along with some basic stage lighting. Yet the limited seating capacity and lack of basic amenities such as restrooms or lounges, and adequate cooling systems doomed them as the feature film, presented in alluring surroundings at the Rex and Strand, with organ or orchestra accompaniment, became the norm for entertainment.

The Lyric (Rialto, Omar, Criterion, etc.) ~

The first of five motion picture theatres built on the principal business block of East Main, between Church and Liberty Streets, opened in April 1909. Located at 136 East Main (later renumbered 140), in half the street level area of a larger building, the Lyric began its long history of name changes within a year after its opening. In rapid succession it became the Majestic, the Tivoli, and the Bijou (not to be confused with the Grand, which also became the Bijou); then for several years it was the Rex, which was dropped when the "new" and much larger Rex opened in 1917. During World War I and into the 1920s it was the Rialto. At the very end of the silent era, it was the Strozier, the Princess, the Omar, and the Ritzy! In the early 1930s, the Wilby-Kincey chain took over the theatre and gave it a final identity: the Criterion. In spite of its small size and travails, the theatre remained in business for some thirty years.

The Lyric seated slightly over 300, and in spite of having only a narrow, shallow stage, it featured a variety of vaudeville acts and even modest chorus lines. Stage shows were advertised regularly from 1909 until the arrival of talking pictures in 1928. In fact, the type of cut-rate vaudeville that had been booked for some two decades at the theatre (and at several houses of similar size that did not survive) enjoyed its last stand in Spartanburg at the Omar in the late 1920s. When the theatre converted to sound, its photoplayer was removed, and the building was slightly extended toward Dunbar Street. All performance facilities disappeared, a new, unadorned proscenium framed the screen without a curtain, and a "washed air" cooling system was installed at the rear.

The entrance of the theatre was fairly spacious and tiled until the walls were plastered over and given a gilded molding. Like all the theatres on Main Street, this one had a bulb-studded sign that extended over the sidewalk. But unlike the Rex and Strand, the Lyric had only a tiny lobby and no restroom facilities. In the 1930s, a marquee with flashing colored bulbs was installed, giving its gilded, paneled entrance a more glamorous effect. Just before the opening of the new Palmetto in 1940, the space was converted into a women's apparel store. When the entire building was demolished in the late 1980s (more than forty years after the Criterion had closed), the old décor was vividly exposed on the side of the adjacent Smith's Drug Store with the outlines of the elevated theatre floor clearly preserved and the gilded masks of tragedy and comedy on the side panels still gleaming. Apparently, it attracted little curiosity, and the elements soon began to erase the surviving, ghostly remnants of the theatre of many names.

The Grand (Bijou) ~

The Grand was the second movie-vaudeville house to be built on the principal business block of East Main Street, and with its opening in 1910 Spartanburg's incipient theatre district moved from Magnolia and North Church to the area where most of the theatres would be clustered for the next half-century. But the only evidence of its existence are the newspaper advertisements that appeared over a period of some fourteen years and old photographs of Main Street that show its electric sign extending out over the sidewalk, with a curious pair of lighted crescents ornamenting either side of the entrance. It was built during the boom in theatre construction spurred by the rapid development of motion pictures as a major form of popular entertainment. The theatre was described in the *Herald* as "double the size" of other vaudeville-movie theatres in town (meaning the Lyric and the short-lived Royal Palace and Royal), and its owner, Lawrence Lester, proclaimed it "the house beautiful." Located on the south side of the street at number 139, it occupied what was later to be the western half of McClellan's Five and Ten. The building itself did not extend entirely to Broad Street, so that the actual theatre space could have been only slightly larger than that of the Lyric. The Sanborn Insurance Maps confirm its precise location and size, and the most reliable documentation of its seating capacity place it in the 300-350 range on the main floor. A photoplayer theatre organ was installed to accompany silent films, and like all of Spartanburg's theatres, it prospered during World War I, when it could draw on the additional audience of thousands of trainees at Camp Wadsworth. While the Grand was not actually "double the size" of the Lyric, it may well have seemed more spacious because of a higher ceiling and even a small balcony (whose seats might not have been included in Cahn-Hill estimates). When Lawrence Lester sold the theatre in 1915, the name was changed to the Bijou.

The Lester (Strand) ~

Although it was known as "The Strand" for more than three decades, this very special theatre on the north side of East Main opened in 1913 as "The Lester," namesake and dream house of Lawrence Lester, Jr.,

EVERYONE KNOWS NOW!

The STRAND is the SECOND RUN THEATRE of Spartanburg

BRINGING BACK THE CHOICE OF THE BIG PICTURES

THE STRAND	STRAND	ALL SEATS
Gets its Pictures from the Four Largest Studios in the World. Metro-Goldwyn-Mayer Paramount Pictures Warner Brothers First National Pictures		15c ALL HOURS

Spartanburg's own movie impresario who had opened the first "electric" theatres on Magnolia Street and moved on to Main Street in 1910 to build the Grand. It is probable that Lester himself had considerable input into the actual design of his finest theatre. The large ads he placed in local newspapers spelled out all its amenities—modern heating and ventilation, fire exits, wide aisles, and "seats of comfort." This time a new theatre lived up to its hype.

Constructed on the site of several small stores and shops, the Lester was the largest building on East Main between the Southern Railroad crossing and Liberty Street. It was also the first structure in the area to extend through the block to what would become an extension of Dunbar Street. It had about 650 seats on the steeply raked, wooden main floor and perhaps 100-150 more in the balcony at the rear of the house. The Lester was, of course, double the size of the Lyric and Grand, but because of the narrow overhang of the balcony and the high overhead ceiling it seemed even larger than it really was. Just inside the double pair of gilded entrance doors were wide carpeted stairways on either side that led to the balcony, the manager's office, and the projection booth; the wide inner lobby was flanked by restrooms. There were two aisles, with a middle section of fourteen or fifteen seats and narrower side sections at right and left of perhaps six seats. The side walls were distinguished by very large damask-covered panels (faded burgundy in the last years of the theatre); overhead were six or eight bronze metal chandeliers of the "inverted pan" type, with an outer circle of bulbs; on the walls were sconces with translucent shades. The proscenium, outlined in gilt, was relatively small, so that the screen and its black masking filled the entire area except for a few feet of the front curtain when it was drawn. Whatever backstage dressing facilities that had existed in the early years had disappeared with the conversion to sound in 1929 and the installation of a "washed-air" cooling system, and a platform stage had been constructed where the organ and, later, a photoplayer had been installed. This served for guest appearances and talent shows.

In 1915, the Lester was sold to the Carolina Amusement Co., E. J.

Sparks became its manager, and the theatre's name was permanently changed to "The Strand." A new organ (probably one of the larger photoplayers) was installed in 1917, reportedly at a cost of $10,000 (an enormous expense at that time). In the mid-1920s, the Strand became part of the vast Publix-Paramount chain. In 1927, a new Wurlitzer photoplayer was installed, only to be discarded when the theatre was wired for sound films in the summer of 1929.

The Lester/Strand would exist for some thirty-three years in downtown Spartanburg as testimony to Lawrence Lester's understanding, perhaps instinctive, that theatres should complement the stage performance or film exhibition to enhance the theatrical experience. As the Strand, the theatre underwent periodic refurbishing, eventually reaching a state of benign neglect. Still, its essential architectural elements

This is Main Street Spartanburg on a Saturday in 1946. The Strand theatre, at right, had recently closed. The State Theatre marquee, at left, announces a Gene Autry Western.
—*Courtesy, B&B Studio*

remained intact, its deep red carpet continued to harmonize with the gilded box office, the plaster ornamentation and the damask on the walls. The bulb-studded entrance arch defied the attachment of an obscuring marquee, even after both the State and the Criterion had acquired one. The only noticeable addition was the placement of glass display frames at either side for stills and poster cards, where originally there had been elaborate plaster design. The building that housed the Lester/Strand is still one of the larger surviving relics of the past on Spartanburg's Main Street. It first became a Lerner's apparel store in 1947, and when downtown retail businesses began to close, it was converted into office space. The brick façade added at that time gives no hint of the theatre's original entrance, but undoubtedly some of the theatre's interior décor still survives beneath sheetrock or other modern materials.

The Rex (State, Capri) ~

On September 11, 1917, the new Rex joined the three theatres already in operation on the principal block of East Main Street. Built by C. L. Henry and operated by him in its early years, it replaced several nondescript store buildings and a large livery stable, and it extended

A
Public
Theatre

Home of
Paramount
Pictures

through the block to Broad Street. With some 850 seats, it was somewhat larger than the Strand, and its lobby space was considerably more ample. Beautifully decorated at the time of its opening, this sparkling new theatre was Spartanburg's leading motion picture theatre for the next decade. Even after the opening of the Montgomery, the Rex remained a premier first-run house until the end of the silent era. Although the theatre employed a musical director and small orchestra at the time of its inauguration, a photoplayer was later installed and, in 1927, a Wurlitzer pipe organ (Opus 1654).

The auditorium was approximately 48 x 78 feet, with a 38-foot lobby, the inner part flanked by small lounges and restrooms. Wide stairways on either side ascended to the balcony. The stage was 23 feet deep from the footlights but not quite large enough to accommodate the types of plays and musicals that had played at the Harris and which would be booked at the Montgomery after 1925. Its stage offerings were also limited by the cramped dressing rooms for performers beneath the stage. But the theatre interior was a feast for the eyes. The seats had cut-velvet panels of burgundy and gold, and the carpets were of the same colors. Wall panels were framed with hand-painted designs, and in the center of each was the logo of the Rex edged in black and gold on a grey panel. The proscenium also featured detailed painted designs and rich stage hangings. Over the orchestra and the large balcony were round metal chandeliers almost identical to those in the Strand; these were the only element that did not totally harmonize with the theatre's décor. A plaster cornice ran the length of the auditorium to the proscenium edge, and it is possible that behind this were wiring and sockets for cove lighting.

The closing of the Rex in May of 1929 was assumed temporary, so that the theatre could be wired for sound films; however, the theatre would be unused except for a few special live performances for almost five years. Since the stock market crash was several months in the future, it is probable that other economic factors contributed to the prolonged closing. The theatre would finally reopen in 1934 as the State, under the management of the Palmetto Amusement Company. Whereas the Rex had been decorated in rich colors with detailed hand-painted or stenciled designs on the walls and proscenium, the remodeled house was painted in shades of green and gray. The burgundy front curtain remained, but the seats with their cut-velvet back panels were replaced with less luxurious, solid bentwood backs. The old box office was replaced by a slightly smaller one in the 1930s style. Inside, the hatcheck room gave way to extra seats at the back of the orchestra section. The exit levels on either side of the stage (which had been reached via steps and a platform that extended outward on each side of the orchestra and organ area) were lowered to floor level, and a few rows of side seats were added. This may have taken away some of the dressing room area beneath the stage. The Rex once probably had a standee rail at the rear, and this area was filled with two or three rows of additional seats. On the second floor of the theatre, directly over the main lobby, was a space that opened on offices but that could have easily served as an additional lobby area for patrons. At the rear of the balcony, a single seat from the Rex remained as a reminder of the elegance that once prevailed. Both the Wurlitzer organ and the photoplayer were removed, and their fate is currently unknown.

The new State became Spartanburg's "B" house, showing the potboilers of Hollywood studios, and on weekends there was an inevitable western featuring Buck Jones, Tom Mix, and other popular cowboy stars, accompanied by a serial. In the late 1930s and early 1940s, the management regularly booked second-rate vaudeville shows, which were accompanied by a totally unmemorable film. With the opening of the Palmetto in 1940, the State became a second-run theatre like the Strand and began to book major films that had shown at the Carolina a few months earlier.

The theatre got a new lease on life in the 1950s when it once again became a first-run house after the Wilby-Kincey monopoly ended and the block-booking practice of Hollywood studios was eliminated by court order. A new management took over, and moviegoers found themselves returning to a house that some had avoided for years to see the films of Rock Hudson, Jane Wyman, and Doris Day; also, thanks to the relatively wide proscenium bequeathed by the

The State (the old Rex) became Spartanburg's "B" movie house in 1934, then showed first-run films in the 1950s, and later became The Capri. —*Courtesy, B&B Studio*

designers of the Rex, a wide screen was installed without compromising the architectural integrity of the building. In 1970, the theatre was redecorated in the manner in vogue at the time—hanging drapes over dingy walls in lieu of repainting. The proscenium was repainted, losing some of its original stenciled details, but no structural changes were made. With comfortable new seats and new air-conditioning, the State—now renamed the Capri to suggest a different image—showed promise of surviving the competition of shopping-mall theatres for a few more years. Unfortunately, a late-night fire did extensive damage to the roof and auditorium a short time later. Although the basic structure remained intact, the owners decided not to replace the roof and undertake an expensive interior restoration. The space was gutted, eliminating the last of the original four movie-vaudeville houses clustered in what had once been the very heart of Spartanburg's business district. Only the original façade of the theatre remains.

The Montgomery (Carolina) ~

The luxurious Montgomery Theatre, an integral part of the new ten-story office building on the northeast corner of North Church and St. John streets, opened on Friday, October 16, 1925, providing Spartanburg with a well-equipped venue for live theatre for the first time in almost five years. On the opposite corner the remaining sections of the Harris theatre, whose stage had been razed in 1920, still stood as a reminder to older Spartans of its past glory.

The sparkling new theatre opened with little fanfare but offered a full season of new touring musicals, plays, and vaudeville. Strangely, a theatre organ was not installed, even though organ chambers had been provided in the faux upper boxes, conduits installed, and a bid placed for a Wurlitzer. The very few silent films that were booked were accompanied by the theatre's orchestra of local musicians or, on one or two occasions, by a pianist in the orchestra pit. In 1926 the theatre became part of the vast Publix-Paramount chain, and both Vitaphone (on disk) and Movietone (on film) sound equipment were installed to enable the theatre to show the many Vitaphone shorts being released by Warner Brothers and the newsreels with sound on film. But the theatre remained principally a venue for live performances, and between 1926 and 1928, it gave Spartanburg its last feast of touring professional shows. With the revolutionary release of *The Jazz Singer* in late 1927, the talkie age had begun. The film opened for a week at the Montgomery on September 18, 1928, and from that point on the theatre was Spartanburg's prime first-run motion picture house. Fully staged touring musicals and plays would gradually become less frequent at the theatre—though vaudeville would remain a weekly staple on weekends until the late 1930s.

The Montgomery provided the ultimate "magic" for the theatregoer, especially in its first two decades, and no theatre in the Carolinas could

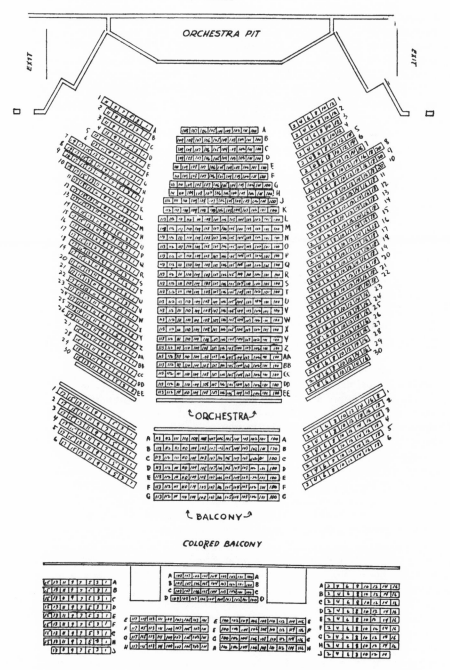

STAGE

ORCHESTRA PIT

EXIT

EXIT

ORCHESTRA

BALCONY

COLORED BALCONY

Ushers were given copies of the seating plan of the Carolina to help them place reserved seat ticket holders in their correct rows. The original seats in the Montgomery were numbered and the row indicated on the aisle seats. When the theatre was refurbished in 1941 and new seats installed, no one seems to have given any thought to stage performances with reserved seats. The new seats lacked numbers and on the rare occasion when a play was booked, the staff had to laboriously mark the row and seat numbers on the floor in chalk. —*Courtesy, author's collection* boast a more congenial design. At first, there was no exterior box office at the entrance, and patrons could buy their tickets for live performances in advance at the adjacent drugstore or at an interior box office in the long, slanting arcade that led to the foyer or inner lobby entrance. The marble-walled hallway, with its vaulted ceiling, cove lights, and series of hanging brass candelabra provided a luxurious introduction to the theatre itself. A triple pair of French doors at the left end of the hallway marked the entrance into the inner lobby, with its marble walls, bronze sconces, and an overhead well that looked up to the mezzanine level, where the ceiling was decorated with delicate, gilded frieze work.

On either side were stairs leading down to the spacious lounges and restrooms and up to the mezzanine and lower balcony. There was a large coatroom at the right of the lobby and a theatre office, with connection to the interior box office at left. On the mezzanine level were additional checkrooms, which would later be used as an ushers' dressing room and a supply room. The manager's private office was discretely off the stairway on one side, and on the other, a door provided access to the upper balcony stairs and the projection booth. Outside, at the rear, were a separate box office and a pair of doors opening on the wide, steep stairway that led to the upper segregated balcony.

A distinctive feature of the interior was the wood paneling that ran down each side of the auditorium almost to the height of the balcony. Undoubtedly this enhanced the acoustics, while providing one of the most eye-pleasing elements of the décor. The proscenium was 36 feet wide and was framed by two levels of stage boxes—the lower ones functional and the upper level designed as organ chambers. A brass rail outlined a sunken orchestra pit (with velvet hangings in the early years). The lighting features were distinctive, with leaded stained glass soffits under the balcony, and a cluster of six chandeliers—each a basket of crystal beads and pendants—set against a gilded plaster grill over the auditorium. There were also provisions for cove lighting above the side walls (with three circuits for multicolored effect) and in the lobby.

The theatre's stage was some thirty feet deep and extended 13 feet on either side of the 36-foot proscenium, for a total width of 62 feet. At stage right, there was a lighting board for both the stage and the auditorium, and on the same side was a large room for storing a supply of stage hangings and the white grand piano that was used for vaudeville and big band performances (and kept in tune by Case Brothers Music House). The backstage area provided ample dressing room facilities even for the larger operetta casts that performed at the theatre frequently in the late 1920s. On three levels off stage right were individual dressing rooms for leading performers. These were outfitted with white wicker furniture, including a chaise lounge for the female star. Beneath the stage were separate dressing rooms and baths for the men's chorus and the women's chorus, as well as a large scenery workshop and a special retiring room for the musicians.

In 1932, the Wilby-Kincey Company took over the management. They changed the name to the Carolina and replaced the original copper marquee with a new, more conspicuous one bordered with flashing bulbs. The interior box office was closed and a new freestanding, gilded one placed at the street entrance. This completed the picture of the Carolina that two or more generations of Spartans would remember. In 1941, some months after the opening of the Palmetto, the theatre was closed for a week for an almost complete refurbishing (only the second, segregated balcony was untouched). New blue and green carpet was laid and more comfortable seats, upholstered in dark green, were installed. A few decorations and stage hangings were replaced but no structural changes resulted except for the unnecessary elimination of the gilded friezes over the mezzanine and foyer. When a cinemascope screen became obligatory in 1953, it was easily placed within the wide proscenium and no structural damage was inflicted to the décor. This did, however, put an end to the presentation of fully staged productions in the house. The old flat screen was on counter weights and could be quickly lifted into the flies, and the single speaker horn was pushed upstage or to one side. Now the wide, curved screen was permanently fixed in place and required three speaker horns.

When segregation ended, the balcony for black patrons was simply closed off and at times business declined to the point that the lower balcony was no longer in use. In the early 1970s, the Carolina was given an ill-advised refurbishing, apparently in an attempt to make it resemble a typical mall cinema, even though single-screen downtown theatres had disappeared or closed all over the United States. Unnecessary damage was inflicted on the auditorium, where the orchestra pit was covered over and the railing removed; the paneled wood standee railings (which duplicated the design of the paneled walls and contributed to the superior acoustics) were simply knocked out. The six chandeliers disappeared, and the gilded grill where they had hung was painted over in a dull gray. The walls were hung with fabric, and new seats complete with the obligatory soft drink holders were installed. Some of the marble wall of the lobby was removed to increase its size, and the curtained French doors were replaced with flimsy louver doors. Over the mezzanine well a cheap "modern" light fixture replaced the sky-blue dome with its floral edging. One of the oddest changes was the reduction of the men's lounge to half its original size. At considerable expense, a new marquee and box office changed the familiar look of the street entrance. But by this time the shop windows in the Montgomery building along the front had been blocked up, and no supporting businesses of any kind remained in the area. Not long after these hideous transformations the Carolina closed, its original décor sadly damaged and its future restoration made more complicated than it might have been. It remains the sole survivor among Spartanburg's theatres.

The Palmetto ~

By the time the Palmetto was built in 1940 in an art moderne (or "futuristic," as the exhibitors preferred) style, the function of most small or middle-sized theatres was simply to exhibit films—though comfort and an aura of luxury for the patrons were still considered essential. This new (and final) theatre for downtown Spartanburg, designed by architect Earl G. Stilwell, replaced some run-down establishments on the prime northwest corner of East Main and North Liberty Streets, and the actual interior design was determined by the relatively cramped piece of real estate. Nevertheless, it had a slightly larger seating capacity (850) than the old Strand because of its larger balcony, which contained a rear section for segregated black audiences (and an ingenious side entrance that provided access to the same box office that served the front entrance). There were no stage facilities at all, and the simple proscenium

In 1965, the Palmetto Theatre was promoting "Major Dundee," a western spectacle already disowned by director Sam Peckinpah. —*Courtesy, Tommy Acker*

The Palmetto Theatre featured George Murphy in "Ringside Maisie" on this evening in 1941, a few months after its opening as Spartanburg's new "B" house. —*Courtesy, Tommy Acker*

served merely as a frame for the screen and front curtain. The architect, like the owners, did not anticipate that within a dozen years or so cinemascope and wide-screen films would be introduced and that the standard picture ratio (1:1.33) would become increasingly rare. Unlike the older theatres with stages, the Palmetto could never effectively accommodate the wide-screen formats. The "widescreen" that was eventually devised looked decidedly undersize—since it was merely the old screen with the top masking lowered. The theatre did, however, prove to be a good venue for 3-D films during their brief popularity.

At the time of its opening, the stylish Palmetto was a marvelously comfortable place to see a movie. Although it resembled many other theatres built in the late 1930s and early 1940s, it did not feature any of the more obtrusive modernistic touches that quickly dated so many of its kind. The carpet, with a light geometric design against a red background, was deep; the seats were relaxing and staggered to provide an unobstructed view of the screen from any location; and a glistening metallic curtain (operated automatically from the projection booth) opened and closed dramatically at the beginning and end of a feature film. The dark red walls were decorated with bold abstract murals painted on acoustically-treated plaster that were one of the trademarks of futuristic interiors. A single carpeted stairway led up to the balcony level and a mezzanine lobby area. Only the rather cramped restrooms off this lobby seemed inappropriate for a theatre of this class. Like the Carolina, the Palmetto also employed a full corps of uniformed ushers to accompany patrons to their seats and police the aisles in its early years.

In the mid 1950s, Kerr McBride became manager. He attempted to maintain profitability in a theatre that was in dire need of a thorough refurbishing. With the assistance of the Spartanburg Fine Film Committee, he was able to book dozens of unusual films that would never have played in town otherwise and to acquire a loyal and appreciative audience for the usual Wednesday-Thursday bookings. As the carpet became worn beyond use in the lobby and aisles, cheap linoleum tiles replaced it; the front curtain had lost most of its metallic sheen and creaked when it was opened and closed; and the age of uniformed ushers was long gone.

Like hundreds of downtown theatres across America, the Palmetto survived a while longer with karate and X-rated films, and in the process it became terra incognita for many Spartans who had once frequented it. For years, it remained closed as the building deteriorated further behind the attractive movie-deco façade. In the early years of the new century, the roof collapsed and in June 2003, the entire building was bulldozed to make way for a new office building.

The Dunbar (Union) and the Ritz ~

After the demise of Spartanburg's first "colored" theatre, Lawrence Lester's Globe on South Liberty Street, several other theatres opened on North Church for black patrons. These short-lived movie theatres did not (or could not) advertise their films in the local newspapers, so the record of their existence lies in city directories and Sanborn Insurance Maps that document their precise locations. Around 1926, a new theatre called the Dunbar opened on Short Wofford Street in an area of African-American businesses sandwiched between North Church and Magnolia streets. In the early 1930s, it was converted to sound and renamed the Union. The seating capacity of the narrow auditorium was about 350, and the entrance bore a passing resemblance to the Strand's, with an arch studded with electric bulbs. In other respects, it was more like the Criterion, featuring an ornamented box office set in the center of the entranceway, with double doors on either side. Only by venturing halfway down narrow Short Wofford was it possible to read the displays that proclaimed the film of the day, since the Union had no flashing marquee. The theatre played some of the all-black films released in the 1930s, as well as second and third-run westerns and musicals. The theatre was demolished when St. John Street was extended from North Church to Magnolia in the 1940s.

When the Union closed, a new and larger theatre for black patrons was built outside the core downtown area, at the rear of the Kennedy Free Library. With a capacity of 500, the Ritz was an unpretentious cinderblock structure, with a narrow marquee across its entrance and display cases for one-sheets and movie stills. Its interior, decorated in the theatre-modern style of the day, was inoffensive if not distinctive. This theatre also fell victim to "progress" when Charles Street was extended from Magnolia to circle behind the Spartanburg Court House. Segregation was now ended, and black audiences finally had access to all theatres at the moment their magic was fading and television had become major competition.

Stage Attractions

*T*he following are representative professional stage attractions performed in Spartanburg during the first half of the
twentieth century. The reader should keep in mind that this
extensive list represents only a portion of the hundreds of
plays, musicals, vaudeville shows, and other presentations performed in
Spartanburg theatres over a half-century, but it does provide an accurate
overview, along with some of the most memorable shows. Although the
1907 performance of *Twelfth Night* took place in the Converse College
outdoor theatre, it is included because of the extraordinary cast it
brought to Spartanburg.

In the first two decades of the century, the theatre season ran from
September through May, and some weeks were fully booked. During the
1917-1918 season all the theatres were closed for a period due to a
meningitis threat and for a longer time because of the deadly Spanish flu
epidemic. From the closing of the Harris Theatre in 1920 until the opening
of the Montgomery in 1925, Spartanburg had no stage large enough to
accommodate touring plays and musicals. During that period the only live
professional entertainment (except for an occasional stock company that
performed its repertory under a tent) was vaudeville of different types
that played the Main Street houses along with films.

With the arrival of sound films at the Montgomery in 1928, the
bookings of live shows declined. During the Great Depression, live
vaudeville-type attractions were almost a weekly event at the Carolina,
with plays scheduled only occasionally. The last fully staged professional
production seen on a downtown stage was *Private Lives*, on December 6,
1950.

Sept. 5, 1902
The Telephone Girl (From New York Casino,
comic opera)
Opera House

Oct. 3, 1902
A Colonial Girl ("A Romantic Comedy
Drama-The most Elaborate Scenic
Production
of the season")
Opera House

Oct. 10, 1902
Much Ado About Nothing (Charles B.
Hanford, accompanied by Miss Marie
Drofman)
Opera House

Oct. 29, 1902
At Cozy Corners (Splendid scenery, superb
support, with "pretty, dainty, petite
Adelaide Thurston")
Opera House

Nov. 8, 1902
A Wise Woman ("Deliciously funny comedy,
introducing Marie Lamour")
Opera House

Dec. 9, 1902
Greater NY Minstrels ("Funny comedians,
talented singers, clean dancers, band and
orchestra, parade Tuesday morning")
Opera House

Nov. 6, 1903
Facing the Music (with Henry E. Dixey;
original New York company and scenery)
Opera House

Dec. 3, 1903
Romeo and Juliet (Shakespeare; special
electric effects)
Opera House

Jan. 2, 1904
Railroad Jack ("The Funniest Show on
Earth" – Comedy Drama in 4 Acts)
Opera House

Jan. 4, 1904
"The Knowles" ("Marvelous Scientific
Demonstrations of the Occult Science")
Opera House

Jan. 20, 1904
A Texas Steer (with Milt Barlow, May
Bretonne, and the Texas Steer Quartette)
Opera House

Mar. 16, 1905
Captain Barrington
Opera House

Mar. 20, 1905
Utah (Crescent Comedy Co.)
Opera House

Apr. 17, 1905
The Black Patti Troubadours
Opera House

Apr. 28, 1905
Don Caesar de Bazan ("presented in a
Sumptuous Manner with every Attention
to Detail")
Opera House

Mar. 12, 1906
Buster Brown (Farewell tour, Melville B.
Raymond, with "Master Gabriel")
Opera House

Mar. 14, 1906
Il Trovatore (English Grand Opera Co.,
with contralto Mme. Mantelli)
Opera House

Sept. 19, 1906
Peck's Bad Boy ("clever entertainment
and pretty girls")
Opera House

Sept. 24, 1906
The Terrible Turk
Opera House

Sept. 25, 1906
The Sultan of Sulu (Musical comedy by
George Ade,"21 song hits")
Opera House

Sept. 27, 1906
Human Hearts (W. E. Nankeville –
"abounding in humanity and bubbling over
with joyous comedy")
Opera House

Oct. 1, 1906
Donnelly and Hatfield Magnificent Minstrels
("Startling electrical effects; Big Noonday
Parade and Concert")
Opera House

Jan. 2, 1907
Rip Van Winkle (with Thomas Jefferson,
son of Joseph)
Opera House

Jan. 4, 1907
A Message from Mars ("Faustian dream
sequence")
Opera House

Jan.5, 1907
My Wife's Family (Musical show)
Opera House

Jan. 7, 1907
It's All Your Fault (Edward Selwyn)
(with Charles Stone and Olive Evans)
Opera House

Jan. 10, 1907
Gay New York (" . . .the song "Hinkey Dee"
got exactly four more encores than any
song heard on the local stage this year.")
Opera House

Jan. 14, 1907
Buster Brown (Sold out; standing
room only)
Opera House

Jan. 15, 1907
King of Tramps (comedy in 4 Acts)
Opera House

Jan. 17, 1907
When Knighthood was in Flower ("A rush
for seats when the box-office opened
at Greenewald's")
Opera House

Jan. 21, 1907
My Lady Nell ("A New Thrilling Western
Drama') (standing room only)
Opera House

Jan 24, 1907
Parsifal (with John Lane Connor and
Virginia Keating; "performance begins at
7:45 and practice of signaling beginning
with trumpets is being adhered to")
Opera House

Jan. 31, 1907
Our New Minister (Denman Thompson
and George W. Ryer)
Opera House

Feb. 11, 1907
The Slaves of the Orient ("specialties
between the acts")
Opera House

Feb. 14, 1907
East Lynne (by 7:30 all standing room
was sold and many were turned away)
Opera House

Feb. 25, 1907
The Sweetest Girl in Dixie
Opera House

Mar. 15, 1907
The Clansman (T. Dixon) (advanced
prices: $1.00 - $1.50)
Opera House

Mar. 27, 1907
Our New Minister (with Joseph Conyers
and the original cast)
Opera House

Mar. 28, 1907
Gorton's Famous Minstrels (with grand
street parade)
Opera House

Mar. 29, 1907
The Lyman Twins and Patti Rosa and
Her Trolley Girls
Opera House

Apr. 3, 1907
The Man on the Box (with Max Figman)
Opera House

May 11, 1907
Twelfth Night (Shakespeare) (3:30pm)
(Ben Greet Players, with Ben Greet, Sybil
Thorndike, Sidney Greenstreet, Percy Waram)
Open Air Theatre, Converse College

Oct. 8, 1907
The Red Feather (DeKoven) (first
performance in new theatre and opening
of fall season)
Harris

Oct. 13, 1907
The Black Patti Troubadours
Harris

Oct. 13, 1907
The Rivals (Sheridan) (with Jefferson
brothers)
Harris

Oct. 16, 1907
Richard III (Shakespeare) (small audience
reported)
Harris

Sept. 8, 1908
A Daughter of America (with Olga von
Hatsfeldt and Company of 50/Opening
of 1908-09 season)
Harris

Sept. 14, 1908
Blue Grass (adaptation of Schweitzer's
Epidemic by Augustin Daly) (Demorest
Comedy Co. – 3 nights in repertory)
Harris

Sept. 16, 1908
The Soul Kiss ("big musical sensation")
Harris

Sept. 21, 1908
The Shadow (King Dramatic Co.; play
change nightly; full orchestra)
Harris

Sept. 22, 1908
The Smart Set ("America's Cleverest Colored
Comedians.") (Entire Balcony and Gallery
for Colored People)
Harris

Sept. 30, 1908
Beulah (with Miss Janet Waldrop; "a
fascinating stage picture of southern life;"
dramatized from the stirring romance by
Augusta J. Evans)
Harris

Jan. 4, 1909
Coming Thro The Rye ("The Greatest of
all the Big Musical Comedy Successes")
Harris

Jan 15, 1909
The Cat and the Fiddle (Lyrics and music by
Carlton Lee Colby; 40 people, 21 song hits,
the Elmore Sisters and the Gigantic Cat)
Harris

Jan. 30, 1909
A Knight for a Day ("The Season's Event.
The Roar That Won't Subside—Original
Company of 60 Song Birds")
Harris

Feb. 3, 1909
The Man of the Hour
Harris

Feb. 10, 1909
Creatore and his Band (50 Musicians and
50 Soloists)
Harris

Feb. 11, 1909
A Trip to Africa (The Black Patti Musical
Comedy Co.) (with Mme. Sissieretta Jones
and "Jolly" John Larkins, with large
company of Colored Entertainers)
Harris

Feb. 17, 1909
The Clansman ("4th Season—Witnessed
by over 4,000,000 theatre goers")
Harris

Feb. 18, 1909
The Honeymooners ("New York Musical
Comedy Triumph")
Harris

Oct. 28, 1909
The Money Maker (Wayne Musical Comedy
Company, "repertory changed nightly, new
electric effects")
Harris

Jan. 24, 1910
The Girl of the Golden West (David Belasco)
Harris

Oct. 3, 1910
The Newlyweds ("The great big cheer up
song comedy" – 60 & + people, with
Countess Olga van Harzfeld, J. Rusen,
and Leo Haynes)
Harris

Oct. 7, 1910
The Girl Behind the Counter (musical comedy
with Dick Bernard; presented by Lew Fields)
Harris

Oct. 11, 1910
A Gentleman from Mississippi (Harrison
Rhodes and Thomas Wise)
Harris

Dec. 6, 1910
The Bachelor (Clyde Fitch) (with Mr. Paul
Gilmore)
Harris

Feb. 2, 1911
Buster Brown ("A Show For Children
From 7-10")
Harris

Feb. 11, 1911
A Trip to Africa, The Black Patti Musical
Comedy Company in the Revised Musical
Success")
Harris

Mar. 6, 1911
The Prize Winners ("A Host of Pretty Girls,
Funny Comedians")
Harris

Mar. 8, 1911
The Blue Mouse ("A Farce in Three Acts
from the German")
Harris

Sept. 4, 1912
Common Law ("A. H. Woods Offers a
Dramatization of Robert W. Chambers'
Famous Novel . . . Pulsating with the joys
and sorrows of everyday life")
Harris

Sept. 6, 1912
Naughty Marietta (Victor Herbert) ("Oscar
Hammerstein presents Florence Webber and
Her Original Company of 60 Vocalists")
Harris

Oct. 7, 1912
The Halloween Girls ("Catchy Music,
New Songs, Original Ideas . . .")
Harris

Oct. 10, 1912
45 Minutes from Broadway (George M.
Cohan) ("Catchy Music, Pretty Girls,
a Real Music Play for Real People")
Harris

Nov. 12, 1912
The Bohemian Girl ("A Lavish Pictorial
Production of Balfe's Melodious
Masterpiece")
Harris

Jan. 15, 1913
The "Black Patti" Musical Comedy Co. (with
Sissieretta Jones, the original "Black Patti."
"Entire house except left side of orchestra
reserved for colored people."
25-cents to $1.00)
Harris

Nov. 1, 1913
The Girl of My Dreams (book by Wilbur
D. Nesbit and Otto Hauerbach; music
by Karl Hoschna)
Harris

Dec. 10, 1913
Creatore's Band & the Lamberto Opera
Sextet
Harris

Dec. 12, 1913
The Quaker Girl (cast headed by Victor
Morley) (musical version of *Peg O 'My Heart*)
Harris

Oct. 2, 1914
The Virginian (Bartley Campbell)
Harris

Oct. 12, 1914
Stop Thief (Carlyle Moore and George
M. Cohan) ("the show that put the gay in
gayety," with Bert Leigh and Hazel Burgess)
Harris

Oct. 15, 1914
Peg O' My Heart (J. Hartley Manners)
(an Oliver Morosco production with
Blanche Hall as Peg)
Harris

Oct. 24, 1914
Bringing Up Father
Harris

Nov. 3, 1914
Believe Me (musical satire with Billy
Clifford)
Harris

Nov. 16, 1914
The Movie Girl
Harris

Dec. 8, 1914
The Old Homestead (Denman Thompson)
(celebrated double male quartette, Grace
Church NY Choir of 20 voices, "oceans of
laughter and tears," –matinee and night)
Harris

Dec. 9, 1914
Primrose and Wilson Minstrels
Harris

Dec. 28, 1914
George Evans's *Honey Boy Minstrels*
Harris

Jan. 27, 1915
The Prince of Tonight (Adams, Hough,
and Howard) (Tom Arnold and a cast
of 50, Pony Ballet of wonderful dancers,
Blue & Silver Ballet)
Harris

Feb. 3, 1915
Creatore and His Band
Harris

Feb. 11, 1915
Il Trovatore (opera by Verdi)
(performed by Boston English Opera Co.)
Harris

Feb. 12, 1915
Bought and Paid For (George Broadhurst)
Harris

Mar. 11, 1915
J. C. Coburn's Greater Minstrels
Harris

Mar. 22, 1915
Seven Keys to Baldpate (George M. Cohan)
Harris

Mar. 29, 1915
Neil O'Brien's Minstrels
Harris

Oct. 28, 1916
The Princess Pat (Victor Herbert)
(augmented V. Herbert Orchestra)
Harris

Oct. 31, 1916
The Serenade (Victor Herbert) (Walker
Stevens Co.; Luigi di Francesca, Cond.)
Harris

Nov. 8, 1916
Gus Hill's Follies of 1917
Harris

Nov. 23, 1916
33 Washington Square (musical starring
May Irwin)
Harris

Nov. 27, 1916
Nobody Home (music by Jerome Kern; book
& lyrics by Guy Bolton and Paul Rubens)
(with Charles McNaughton and Zoe Barnett)
Harris

Dec. 1, 1916
Russian Symphony Orchestra, with Carolyn
Cone, "brilliant young American pianist."
Harris

Dec. 5, 1916
The Girl Who Smiles (with Bert Leight
and Hazell Burgen)
Harris

Dec. 11, 1916
Gypsy Love (Lehár) (presented by Andreas
Dippel, with Arthur Albro and Finita
deSoria; Milan Roder, Cond.)
Harris

Jan. 9, 1917
Sarah Bernhardt in scenes from *Cleopatra*
and *Camille*: "Champs D'Honneur," and
"The Husband's Luck."
Harris

Sept. 10, 1917
Don't Lie to Your Wife ("Vaudeville
and Musical Comedy Revue")
Harris

Sept. 24, 1917
Cheating Cheaters ("The brightest and
smartest comedy on any stage anywhere")
Harris

Oct. 1, 1917
Very Good Eddie (Jerome Kern, Schuyler
Green, & Guy Bolton)
Harris

Oct. 2, 1917
Pom-Pom ("Mitzi will steal your heart")
Harris

Oct. 19, 1917
The Garden of Allah ("Stupendous
production; 100 people, Arabs, camels.
Train of eight cars; special excursions
on all railroads")
Harris

Nov. 1, 1917
The Million Dollar Doll ("A Bombardment
of Laugh Bombs Served by a Regiment
of Musical Maids and Mirthful Men")
Harris

Jan. 8, 1918
Keith's Polite Vaudeville ("clean and
clever entertainers marked throughout
by refinement and taste")
Harris

Mar. 25 (and following), 1918
You Know Me Al! (New York 27th
Regiment's all-soldier musical)
Harris

Nov. 14, 1918
As You Were (Camp Jackson all-soldier
musical comedy)
Harris

Oct. 14, 1919
So Long Letty (music by Earl Carroll)
Harris

Oct. 16, 1919
Bringing Up Father in Society
Harris

Oct. 18, 1919
The Better Ole (musical with DeWolf Hopper)
Harris

Oct. 20, 1919
Sometime (music by Rudolph Friml;
book & lyrics by Rida Johnson Young;
presented by Arthur Hammerstein)
Harris

Oct. 24, 1919
Tiger Rose ("melodrama")
Harris

Oct. 28, 1919
Up in Mabel's Room (presented by
A. H. Woods)
Harris

Nov. 3, 1919
Parlor, Bedroom, and Bath (presented
by A. H. Woods)
Harris

Nov. 7, 1919
Mutt and Jeff's Dream
Harris

May 18, 1924
Harry Platt's Keystone Follies (with
Keystone Follies Chorus)
Bijou

Oct. 16, 1925
Al C. Field Minstrels (grand opening
of new theatre)
Montgomery

Oct. 26, 1925
Lady Be Good (musical by George and
Ira Gershwin)
Montgomery

Nov. 6, 1925
The Show-off (George Kelly)
Montgomery

Nov. 27, 1925
George White's Scandals (6th edition;
augmented orchestra and three cars
of gorgeous effects)
Montgomery

Dec. 19, 1925
Lasses White All-Star Minstrels
Montgomery

Jan. 26, 1926
Love-in-a-Mist (Gilbert Emery)
(with Madge Kennedy and Sidney Blackmer)
Montgomery

Jan 27, 1926
George White's Scandals (7th edition;
with "amazing Albertina Rasch Dancing
Girls; exactly as performed in New York's
Apollo Theatre")
Montgomery

Oct. 2, 1926
Love 'Em and Leave 'Em ("rip-roaring
comedy," Kirk Brown Jr. & his players)
Montgomery

Oct. 4,5,6, 1926
The Man Who Came Back (Jules E. Goodman)
(with Irene Hubbard, "melodrama of
modern life")
Montgomery

Oct. 12, 1926
Rose Marie (music by Rudolph Friml; book
by Harbach & Hammerstein; company of 70)
Montgomery

Oct. 13, 1926
The Green Hat (Michael Arlen) (with
Charlotte Walker and Norman Hackett)
Montgomery

Oct. 18, 1926
Will Rogers, plus the De Reszke Singers
Montgomery

Oct. 29, 1926
The Student Prince (Sigmund Romberg)
(chorus of 60)
Montgomery

Nov. 26, 1926
Greenwich Village Follies (cast of 40)
Montgomery

Dec. 6, 1926
Julius Caesar (Shakespeare)
(Robert B. Mandell and Genevieve Hamper)
Montgomery

Dec. 7, 1926
Macbeth (Shakespeare) (Robert B. Mandell
and Genevieve Hamper)
Montgomery

Feb. 21-26, 1927
Three Wise Fools (Austin Strong) ("Dainty
little Edna Park and Associated Players in
the great comedy drama") (schools and
college students 25-cents at matinee)
Montgomery

Mar. 7-8, 1927
The Patsy ("between acts, Johnnie Blowers
and his popular Montgomery Orchestra,
offering the latest and most popular
musical selections")
Montgomery

Oct 3, 1927
Al G. Field Minstrels
Montgomery

Oct. 7, 1927
Ziegfeld's *Kid Boots* (with Pauline Blair
and Charles Williams)
Montgomery

Oct. 20, 1927
The Constant Wife (Somerset Maugham)
(with Lou Tellegen, Charlotte Walker,
and Norman Hackett)
Montgomery

Nov. 9, 1927
Keith Vaudeville & the Montgomery Theatre
Orchestra (3 shows daily at 3-7-9)
Montgomery

Nov. 16, 1927
Keith Vaudeville (8 units plus
Montgomery Orchestra)
Montgomery

Nov. 25, 1927
Earl Carroll Vanities
Montgomery

Dec. 5, 1927
Queen High (musical comedy)
Montgomery

Dec. 13, 1927
Keith Vaudeville
Montgomery

Dec. 16, 1927
Hit the Deck (Vincent Youmans)
("Sometimes I'm Happy," "Hallelujah")
(with Marion Saki; $3.60-$1.20)
Montgomery

Dec. 17, 1927
Lasses White Minstrels
Montgomery

Apr. 27, 1928
The Society for the Preservation of
Spirituals (under auspices of Church
of the Advent)
Montgomery

Nov. 22, 1928
The Desert Song (Sigmund Romberg;
Otto Harbach & Oscar Hammerstein, II)
(with Lillian Wagner)
Montgomery

Feb. 27, 1929
Rio Rita (Tierney, McCarthy, Bolton,
Thompson) (with Peggy Bourne)
Montgomery

Nov. 7, 1929
Good News (DeSylva, Brown and Henderson)
("The Best Things in Life are Free")
Montgomery

Mar. 28-29, 1932
Jack Bigelow's *Musical Misses* ("an RKO
stage band presentation; all girl band,
Nora Luther, WGN radio blues singer,
Barry and De Alba adagio dancers,
Davis and Jefferies, nut comedians")
Carolina

Oct. 6-7, 1933
Girls in Cellophane (vaudeville)
Carolina

Oct. 20, 1933
The Green Pastures (Marc Connelly)
Carolina

Nov. 13, 1933
High-Lites of 1934 (starring Betty Compson)
Carolina

Jan. 4, 1934
La Vie Paree (Greater Marcus Show)
(Midnight Frolic: 11:05pm; "Spectacle
supreme, dashing models and happy art
students, Paris by night" 44cents to $1.50)
Carolina

Jan. 26-27, 1934
Rhythm Aristocrats (RKO Vaudeville unit
& film)
Carolina

Feb. 16-17, 1934
Mildred Harris Chaplin in her *Hollywood
Revue* (& film)
Carolina

Mar. 9-10, 1934
Diamond Revue (& film) ("a vaudeville
presentation; 28 people")
Carolina

Mar. 16, 1934
Broadway Whirl (RKO Vaudeville Unit,
featuring Jack McBride and His 10
Barbarians)
Carolina

Apr. 25, 1934
The Barretts of Wimpole Street (Rudolph
Besier) (with Katherine Cornell, Basil
Rathbone, Orson Welles) ($1.00 to $3.00)
Carolina

Apr. 27-28, 1934
Chatterbox Revue (& film)
Carolina

May 11-12, 1934
Harry Clark's Revue (& film)
Carolina

May 18-19, 1934
Chicago Follies (& film)
Carolina

Jun. 1-2, 1934
Flashes of Art Revue (& film)
Carolina

Sept. 14-15, 1934
Melody Rambles ("a superb vaudeville
presentation")
Carolina

Sept. 21-22, 1934
Henry Santrey commanding his
"Soldiers of Fortune"
(& film)
Carolina

Nov. 2, 1939
Wake Up and Cheer (Pocket edition
of Broadway musical comedy Hellzapoppin;
cast of 30)
Carolina

Nov. 4, 1939
Spices of 1940 (vaudeville) (& film)
State

Nov. 15, 1939
Russ Morgan and His Orchestra (& film)
Carolina

Jan 26, 1940
Phil Spitalny and His Orchestra (& film)
Carolina

May 17, 1940
Vanities of 1940 (Vaudeville, 35 people)
(midnight show and Mar. 18)
State

Dec. 1, 1940
Chas A. Taylor's *Bronze Manikins*
("the World's Premier Colored Stage Show,
stellar cast of 35 colored artists")
(For Adults Only) (Sunday at 12:01:
2 balconies for colored)
Carolina

Dec. 3, 1940
Jan Savitt and His Top Hatters
Orchestra (& film)
Carolina

Dec. 10, 1940
Ina Ray Hutton and Her "All-Male"
Orchestra (& film)
Carolina

Feb. 24, 1941
The Little Foxes (Lillian Hellman)
(Tallulah Bankhead, Frank Conroy)
Carolina

Dec. 17, 1941
Life with Father (Howard Lindsay and Russel
Crouse) (Dorothy Gish and Louis Calhern)
(Matinee & Evening performances)
Carolina

May 1, 1945
Naughty Marietta (Victor Herbert)
Carolina

Jan. 22, 1948
Joan of Lorraine (Maxwell Anderson)
(Diana Barrymore, Robert Wilcox and
Rosemary Prinz)
Carolina

May 10, 1949
O Mistress Mine (Terence Rattigan) (Sylvia
Sidney, John Loder, and Dick Van Patten)
Carolina

May 17, 1950
Zanzy-Barr Revue (Black artists) (11:30pm)
Carolina

May 21, 1950
Dot Blackwell's School of Dance (& film)
(3:20 and 8:00)
Carolina

May 29, 1950
Johnny Olsen's *Ladies be Seated*
(audience participation show, sponsored
by the Lions' Club)
Carolina

Dec. 6, 1950
Private Lives (Noel Coward)
(Tallulah Bankhead, Donald Cook)
(Final fully staged production at theatre)
Carolina

Marion Peter Holt is an Emeritus Professor of Theatre at the City University of New York and has been a visiting lecturer at the Yale School of Drama and Barcelona's Institut del Teatre. A graduate of Wofford College, he was a member of the Converse College faculty for a decade. His fascination for theatre architecture and performance developed when he was a teenage usher *(center above)* at Spartanburg's Carolina Theatre and heard stories about the heyday of touring shows and the early years of motion pictures.

The Hub City Writers Project is a non-profit organization whose mission is to foster a sense of community through the literary arts. We do this by publishing books from and about our community; encouraging, mentoring, and advancing the careers of local writers; and seeking to make Spartanburg a center for the literary arts.

Our metaphor of organization purposely looks backward to the nineteenth century when Spartanburg was known as the "hub city," a place where railroads converged and departed.

At the beginning of the twenty-first century, Spartanburg has become a literary hub of South Carolina with an active and nationally celebrated core group of poets, fiction writers, and essayists. We celebrate these writers—and the ones not yet discovered—as one of our community's greatest assets. William R. Ferris, former director of the Center for the Study of Southern Cultures, says of the emerging South, "Our culture is our greatest resource. We can shape an economic base…And it won't be an investment that will disappear."

Hub City Anthology • John Lane & Betsy Teter, editors
Hub City Music Makers • Peter Cooper
Hub City Christmas • John Lane & Betsy Wakefield Teter, editors
New Southern Harmonies • Rosa Shand, Scott Gould, Deno Trakas, George Singleton
The Best of Radio Free Bubba • Meg Barnhouse, Pat Jobe, Kim Taylor, Gary Phillips
Family Trees: The Peach Culture of the Piedmont • Mike Corbin
Seeing Spartanburg: A History in Images • Philip Racine
The Seasons of Harold Hatcher • Mike Hembree
The Lawson's Fork: Headwaters to Confluence • David Taylor, Gary Henderson
Hub City Anthology 2 • Betsy Wakefield Teter, editor
Inheritance • Janette Turner Hospital, editor
In Morgan's Shadow • A Hub City Murder Mystery
Eureka Mill • Ron Rash
The Place I Live • The Children of Spartanburg County
Textile Town • The Hub City Writers Project
Come to the Cow Pens! • Christine Swager
Noticing Eden • Marjory Heath Wentworth
Literary South Carolina • Edwin Epps
Noble Trees of the South Carolina Upstate • Mark Dennis, John Lane, Mark Olencki